Running
For Girls Like Us

WHAT YOU NEED TO KNOW FOR HAVING
A GREAT TIME RUNNING:

- HOW TO GET STARTED
- TRAINING PLANS
- STRENGTH TRAINING
- HOW TO AVOID INJURIES
- NUTRITION
- GADGETS

By Gloria Safar

Editor: Jenny Bohrman

Cover art and design: Jay French. http://www.JayFrenchStudios.com

ISBN: 978-1477514061

Also by Gloria Safar

"Triathlon For Girls Like Us"

"Triatlón Para Mujeres Como Nosotras" (Spanish edition.)

Coming soon:

"Nutrition For Girls Like Us"

"Strength Training For Girls Like Us"

Contact the author at http://www.gloriasafar.wordpress.com

Table of Contents

To all the moms, sisters, daughters, aunts, nieces, cousins, and dear friends who inspire others to run.

Foreword
by Jenny Bohrman, editor

For most of my life, I've kept fairly active with various sports and outdoor activities, and my natural eating preferences tend to be on the healthy side. Even as a little kid, I was always more than happy to finish my vegetables. In fact, at the age of three, I named my new puppy "Broccoli" after my favorite food. So when Gloria asked me to edit this book, I didn't expect it to introduce me to any wildly new concepts in health and fitness or have a notable influence on my diet and exercise habits.

Well, I couldn't have been more wrong about that. After editing only the introductory chapter, I found myself inspired to begin training for races again. I first started running as senior in high school. Over the next few years, I became competitive and participated in several 5 and 10ks and three halfmarathons. However, towards the end of college and start of graduate school, I fell back considerably in my training.

This book reminded me of how rewarding running is in so many ways. While reading through the chapters Gloria sent me, intending to focus on grammar and syntax, I'd find myself reminiscing about how I felt at my peak running condition. I started craving the runner's high I used to experience so often, the feeling of giving it my all in front of crowds of people on race day, that warm glow of accomplishment I carried with me for days after completing a new distance or crossing another finish line. Each chapter seemed to reinforce the unmistakable connection between physical and mental health, and I gradually accepted that if I wanted to feel as well as I could, I was going to have to put forth the effort.

So while Gloria continued to send me sections of her book, I launched myself back into a regular running routine, and it felt great: I had to scold myself for ever starting to slack. Then, I got to the Nutrition Chapter, and I became inspired all over again. We've all heard it before: avoid highly processed foods. However, it took Gloria's convincing argument against artificial ingredients to get me to genuinely consider shunning things in commercial packaging. One of the messages in that chapter really stood out to me:

If you fill up on highly processed foods, you won't feel full for long. Although you may not be lacking calories, you'll be lacking nutrients, so you'll never effectively curb your appetite. Despite my childhood love for fruits and veggies, I admittedly let my diet slip, along with my exercise, during my later college and grad school years. More often than they should have, my meals consisted of pizza, fries, ice cream, and sugary lattes and cappuccinos, and it became all too easy to "forget" my daily servings of fruits and veggies.

After editing the Nutrition chapter, I began reading the labels on everything I bought, making sure I could recognize and pronounce each ingredient. I started eating a variety of raw fruits and veggies, nuts, seeds, yogurt, and whole grains. At the same time, I bought new sneakers and began building back up to my old running paces and distances. I quickly realized that altering my diet made it enormously easier to fast-forward myself into great running shape. With proper nutrition, I had so much more energy and stamina, and I felt mentally healthier than I had in a long time.

All this got me intrigued about the book's other advice, so I decided to incorporate some strength training into my weekly running routine, before which I had never done. Turned out Gloria was right again: by adding some arm, back and core workouts to my training, running felt even more effortless.

Within the first two months of editing this book, I shed 12 lbs, even though I was consuming more calories per day than when I was eating a lot of sugary, salty, processed foods. The weight really just fell off and seemed to be replaced by a rejuvenating, overall sense of wellbeing.

Today, I'm combining weight training with running six to ten miles three to four times a week, and I'm completely hooked on unprocessed, healthy foods (I think three-year-old me would be proud.) My taste buds have adapted to appreciate simpler flavors, and I lost the urge to snack between meals. I now follow several of Gloria's recipes, which is still a bit shocking to me, because for most of my life I've avoided meals that involve any sort of preparation.

Whether you're brand new to running or racing or returning after a lull, this book will make a terrific motivator and companion. By following the simple yet powerful advice in this book, I feel healthier, mentally and physically, than I ever have, and I'm ready to start entering some races and showing off. I think I may even try to tackle the infamous 26.2 this fall, now that I have this book as my trusted personal trainer.

So much for focusing on grammar and syntax.

Introduction

If you want to start running, increase your running distance, or decrease your running time, this is the book for you!

If you're new to running, I will present you with all the advantages that running can bring into your life, including enhanced health and wellness, an improved sense of self-worth, and a feeling of accomplishment – not only for you, but for your close friends and family as well. If your goal is to add miles or trim your running times, this book will offer you reliable tips and advice.

Drawing from the latest, trusted health and fitness research, I will lay out a progressive training schedule customized to your personal running goals. This book will get you started and help you build up to whatever running distance you would like to achieve. Throughout the book, I will provide plenty of pointers on equipment, nutrition, and technique.

Why walk if you can run? Or maybe you're wondering just the opposite?

Believe it or not, I used to hate running. I could not understand why anyone would want to run simply for the sake of running. Don't get me wrong; I had been running all my life, first playing tennis, then basketball, volleyball, field hockey, and squash, but all the running I did with these sports had, in my mind, served a purpose: I was chasing a ball. But running without anything to chase, without anything chasing me… that, I just couldn't figure out. During an English class I took about four years after moving to the US, I even wrote a paper about marathon running, just to see if I could learn why anyone would willingly put themselves through such an endeavor. About five years later, I met my friend Susan, who loves to run. She was always inviting me to join her, so I finally started tagging along on my inline skates. But skating alongside of her wasn't too much fun for me: I couldn't go very fast, I wasn't getting any exercise, and I never seemed to be enjoying myself as much as she was. I started to wonder to myself, could it really be fun to run? Susan assured me it was, so I finally put away the skates and started running with her. Fast forward about 10 years, and I have six marathons, (seven if you count the one in the Ironman), numerous half marathons, and dozens of 10 and 5k races under my bra.

It took me a little over a year and lots of time and effort to finally like and look forward to running, but I can honestly say that conquering my distaste for running set me free. Today, I couldn't be a happier runner. I enjoy running in any kind of terrain (well, mud–not so much), weather, and time of day. I love looking for new trails and mapping out new running routes while traveling. I've found that running adds so much to any trip: you end up seeing way more than you could ever absorb from walking or driving alone. (Of course, if you add cycling to the mix, it gets even more interesting… but that's another book.)

I certainly hope that this guide helps you discover the freedom, gratification, and health benefits that running can offer you, too. If you are a runner already, I hope this book helps you take that extra step, go that extra mile, shave those extra minutes, try a different approach, or simply derive greater enjoyment from running.

I can assure you that if you end up falling in love with running, like I did; you will feel better physically and mentally and continue to reap health and wellness benefits for years to come.

So, lace up those shoes, and let's get started!

Cheers,

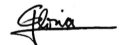

This couple fell in love with running so much
that it became part of their Big Day!

Ch 1

Getting Started

Maybe you never, ever run, maybe you used to run and want to get restarted, or maybe you're currently running, but you'd like to increase your speed or distance. Although you will follow different steps according to your own goals, these steps will abide by the same training principles.

There are many motivations to start running, but there are many, many more excuses not to do so. We will focus on the motivations and ignore the excuses, because I don't believe in any of them! You're not too old, too fat, or too slow to run, even if you have only one leg. I can give you examples of people overcoming almost every excuse in the book, so let's concentrate on what drives us to run and how we can keep those motivations alive.

Research has revealed that the top motivations for running are weight control and mental and physical health.[1, 2] Just ask some runners why they run, and you'll hear things like, "I love to eat; therefore, I run," or, "I don't want to gain those freshman 15," or, "It's cheaper than a shrink" (with all due respect to psychiatrists, especially my sister-in-law). All of these reasons sound good to me! Personally, I really like the feeling of accomplishment I get after a run. Additionally, running provides me with a change of scenery and helps me clear my head when I'm troubled by something. In the winter, when it's really cold and I'm getting cabin fever, there's nothing like a nice outdoor jog to refresh my body and mind. Finally, I like the fact that running allows me to indulge in my favorite foods without a terribly guilty conscience.

Unfortunately, it's a bit harder for most people to find motivations to continue running after they've started. If you're receiving support or encouragement from family and friends to run, then you've already got a head-start on solid dedication.[3, 4] Social support is a key factor in maintaining a level of physical activity in your life. If you are the only one in your social network who runs or wants to run, you can nag – I mean, recruit – friends and relatives to become your running buddies. For my own friend, Susan, it took quite some nagging to convince me to run with her, but I'm very grateful for her efforts!

Here are a few sources of running buddies/support:

- Friends
- Family (if the kids are too young, they can bike with you)
- Coworkers
- Dogs
- Running clubs
- Online running forums

You may need social support before you can gain the sense of well-being that regular exercise provides, so make sure you find some if it's hard for you to go out on your own. As soon as you start feeling the mental and physical benefits that running brings about, you'll be hooked!

Here is the story of how Maureen McCutcheon got into running:

I did not start running until I was 43 years old. I had three children and had just become a stay-at-home mom after the birth of my third child. Once my youngest child started preschool, I wanted to lose weight. I started running with another mom who had a child in my son's class. I found running really relaxing and enjoyed the time to myself. I found running to be good for me both mentally and physically. My first road race was in 2004: the Westfield Turkey Trot. Since then I have done many 5k and 5-mile races. I have also done 4 half marathons and finished the NYC Marathon twice. My last marathon was in November 2010. Now I have just been running to keep in shape. I do about two 3-5 mile runs a week, plus, a 1-mile run to the YMCA and back twice a week.

My family is very supportive. I am not a fast runner – basically, a 10-minute miler. So training for a marathon took up a lot of my time. During the week, I would train while my children were at school and my husband was at work. On the weekends, I would try to go out early and not interfere with the plans for the day. With three children involved in sports and activities, it can get really crazy. My husband and children were so proud of me that we always found a way to work it out.

Running is a wonderful, rewarding experience. Start out gradually. I did not start until later in life and before that I could not run even a half-mile. I truly enjoyed seeing myself progress. You will hit hurdles; I remember getting past three miles as a very big hurdle. I could not imagine that I would ever complete a marathon, and still can't believe I did it. It was such a great feeling, and a great example to set for my children. (In the picture you can see Maureen and her son at a local Turkey Trot race)

I found that having a running partner is very beneficial. There are so many times I would have missed a run, just out of laziness, but knowing that my friend was expecting me would help me get up and get out.

Benefits of Regular Exercise

Regular exercise has many benefits for the body, including decreased susceptibility to various chronic diseases like obesity, Type II diabetes, diabetes mellitus, metabolic syndrome, and breast cancer.[5, 6] Moreover, regular exercise can lower your heart rate, LDL (a.k.a., "bad" cholesterol), blood pressure, fasting glucose, and triglycerides, while increasing your HDL ("good" cholesterol). Hopefully, you know your own numbers for those measurements; if you don't, it will be a good idea to find out. Here is a table with the measurements and their normal, or healthy, ranges. Check your numbers and either brag about them or try to get them within normal levels and *then* brag about them!

Physiological Parameters in Relation to Benefits from Regular Exercise

	Normal Range	Today	Goal
BMI*	18.5 - 24.9		
Resting Heart Rate	60 - 100 bpm		
Blood Pressure	< 120/80 mmHg		
Total Cholesterol	< 200 mg/dl		
HDL	> 40 mg/dl		
LDL	< 100 - 129 mg/dl		
Triglycerides	< 150 mg/dl		
Fasting Glucose	60 - 99 mg/dl		

* Body Mass Index (BMI) is calculated by dividing body weight in kg by height in m²

Additionally, Ellen Seuffert, R.N., F.N.P, from Westfield Family Practice in New Jersey, recommends having your iron levels checked before engaging in any athletic training. She also advises to pay attention to calcium and vitamin D levels. "Depending on your weekly mileage, the severity of your menstrual bleeding and other personal health issues, supplements may be of value, though many women require none whatsoever," she adds.

For improved health, the American College of Sports Medicine (ACSM) recommends that most adults exercise on a regular basis.[7] The minimum dose suggested is 30 minutes of moderate cardiovascular exercise five days a week, for a total of 150 minutes a week. But if you are going to be running, which is considered vigorous exercise, then you can get started with just 20 minutes three days a week, for a total of 75 minutes a week. Of course, you can always combine moderate and vigorous exercise.

In any case, your goal should be to reach a total calorie deficit of 500 to 1000 per week. Or, you may want to push yourself even harder: according to Dr. Josh Palgi, a professor of physical education at Kean University in Union, NJ, if you want to increase physical fitness and maintain a healthy body weight, your total calorie deficit due to physical activity should be at least 2000 per week.

To all this Seuffert adds: – "Good physical fitness involves forethought, patience, consistency and persistence." She recommends exercising most days of the week, and encourages her patients to stick to it and avoid the typical excuses. She also shares some advice she gives herself every day before working out: "The hardest part of exercise is the first five minutes; then you are good to go."

Dose of Exercise to Improve and Maintain Physical Fitness and Health

Goal	Intensity	Frequency	Min. Calorie Deficit*
Improve and maintain physical fitness and health	Moderate	5 x a week 30 min a day	500-1000
Improve and maintain physical fitness and health	Vigorous	3 x a week 20 min a day	500-1000
Increase physical fitness and maintain healthy body weight	Vigorous (with some moderate)	5 x a week 40-60 min a day	2000
One mile walked or ran equals ~100 calories			

If your goal is to start a running program for health benefits, depending on your exercise background, your week could look like this:

Intensity	M	T	W	Th	F	Sa	Su
Moderate	Off	30' E	30' E	Off	30' E	30' E	30' E
Combo Mod/ Vig	Off	30' E	20' R	30' E	Off	20' R	20' E
Vigorous	Off	20' R	Off	20' R	Off	Off, or XT	20' R
E: Easy (walk/run, walking more than running). If you have no exercise experience, one or two of these days may be replaced by a strength training session (more on this later)							
R: Run (or jog)							
XT: Cross Train (any exercise that is not as strenuous as running or where the body is partially supported, not limited to swimming, cycling, rollerblading, and cross-country skiing)							

We will talk more about schedules in the next chapters; this is just a sample to show you that you don't have to run seven miles a day every day to get the benefits of regular exercise.

If you are already a runner and want to increase your fitness level, then, yes, you may need to run five or more miles nearly every day of the week. I'll have a training schedule for you too, with progressive exercises and recovery weeks that will take you safely to your desired goal.

If improved health isn't enough of an incentive for you to pick up running, there are plenty of other initial motivations to choose from, such as enhanced mood, increased muscle tone, and a better social life. Hopefully, you will begin to see that the combined benefits of running outweigh the drawbacks.

Why Run?

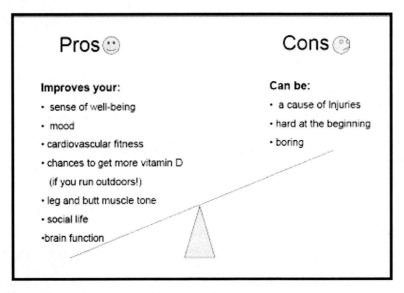

The simple fact is there are many more pros than cons associated with starting a running program, and the cons can be easily tackled. While it's true that increasing the intensity of a workout can lead to injuries, if you start slowly and follow the training principles that we will discuss later, you should be able to stay injury-free. Running can be difficult at first, but as you gradually build speed and distance and improve your cardiovascular health, it will get easier and easier (you might even start experiencing that legendary "runner's high!") And if you're worried that running will be boring, well, you've got a point there, but again, it's something that can be overcome.

When I first started running, I would get very upset if my portable radio didn't have fresh batteries (yes, this is how long I've been running – since before MP3 players and iPods!) However, as I grew more comfortable with running, I slowly got over my dependency on my radio, and actually started to leave it at home. You can treat boredom and monotony with good music (which is a bit easier with today's technology), or better yet, good company. Find a running buddy: you might be surprised to discover your runs ending before your conversations! If you prefer to run alone, there are many other gadgets out there today to keep you motivated/entertained while running (we'll talk more about gadgets later too!).

So, you've decided to start running? Congratulations!! Now let's talk about what you need to get started, such as shoes, how to maximize your results, and how to keep injuries at bay. To make sure you are absolutely physically ready to start a progressive running program, take a look at the PAR-Q and YOU questionnaire at the end of the chapter. Answering this questionnaire will give you the peace of mind that you are fully prepared for the challenge. Of course, you are always encouraged to consult your doctor for additional advice about how and when to start a new exercise routine.

Equipment and Running Technique

Shoes:

I'm sure you have a pair of sneakers in your shoe rack. The questions are: (1) Are those shoes the right type for you? (2) How old are those sneakers? A common source of running injuries is wearing the wrong pair of shoes. Therefore, let's take some time to select the right sneaker for your foot type.

Most running shoes come geared for arch type: high arch, neutral, or low arch. People with high or low-arched feet have an altered foot strike, which creates a misalignment of the ankle and knee joint and may lead to foot or knee injuries. Research has shown that this misalignment can be treated by the use of orthotics and/or shoes designed to compensate for low or high arches.[8] I would

advise you to visit your local running store to have your foot type checked and try different styles and brands of sneakers until you find ones that best fit your needs. These running stores have employees that are trained to assist you in this matter.

David, the manager of my local running store, The Running Company, (TRC) says that the first thing they ask a new costumer to do is walk back and forth barefoot so they can observe the way his or her feet interacts with the ground. Some running stores, TRC inclusive, even have a treadmill with a camera that records your foot strike. After analyzing the way you walk/run, David will carefully measure your feet to find your true size, which will be half a size to a full size bigger than what you're accustomed to, in order to accommodate foot displacement and swelling during running. (By the way, it's a good idea to go shoe shopping at the end of the day, when your feet are most swollen.) Based on that information, along with your foot shape (e.g., the arch), he will bring you two or three different shoe models so you can test them out and choose the one that feels best.

If you have no access to these kinds of stores, you can send your used running/walking shoes to the national retailer, Road Runners Sports. They will analyze the wear of your old shoes in order to determine the type of footwear that's most appropriate for you.

If you already own a pair of running sneakers, ask yourself how old they are. The wear and tear of the shoes will be a factor in the amount of cushioning they will provide you while running. If you don't remember how long you've had your running shoes, I would advise you to get a new pair and save the old ones for gardening or rainy days. Research has shown that running shoes' cushioning and their ability to protect your feet from the constant impact of running decreases after 300[9] to 500[10] km (~200-320 mi). If you run about ten miles a week, this translates to five to eight months' time.

The lifespan of your running shoes will also depend on the type of sneaker, the surfaces you run on, your weight, and whether/how often you wear the shoes outside of running, among other things. David, Manager of The Running Company, recommends having two pairs of running shoes if you run on consecutive days. Alternating sneakers will allow the materials in each pair return to their original state of cushioning before your next run. This will make them last longer, too, says David.

What about barefoot or minimal shoe running? There are a lot of anecdotal accounts of runners curing their chronic pains and injuries by switching from conventional running shoes to minimalist shoes, or losing the shoes altogether. However, according to Dr. Daniel Lieberman and colleagues at Harvard University,[11] barefoot and minimalist shoe runners tend to have a mid-foot or front-foot strike, in contrast to the rear-foot strike most common among runners. Landing on the mid to front part of the foot decreases the impact with which the foot hits the ground, due to the dynamics of the feet's movements. Traditional running shoes tend to have a cushion in the heel area, allowing for a rear-foot strike that would be uncomfortable for a barefoot or minimalist shoe runner. This foot landing preference could be the explanation for reduced cases of lower leg and foot injuries among barefoot and minimalist shoe runners. Therefore, if you do not have a mid- to front-foot strike, minimalist shoes or no shoes may not work as well for you.

Personally, I have four pairs of running shoes that I wear for different terrains and distances. Two of these are for trail running (I wear one pair only if it's muddy and try to keep the other "fairly" clean). I like to wear trail running shoes off-road, because they have more traction than road running shoes. They also have a protective, shock-absorbent sole to shelter your feet from rocks and roots. Some trail running shoes are waterproof, and you can also find them in the minimalist variety, which are lightweight but still adequately protective.

The second type of shoe I wear is a road running shoe with medium support. I like the Asics 2000TM series (also for trail running). They have just the right amount of cushion for my long runs. They come in different widths: I use the D width, which provides a nice wide area for my toes and minimizes blisters. I have used this brand for the last nine years, thanks to the recommendation of a shoe specialist, and I still love these shoes. I had tried several different makes before with no luck (blisters galore, uncomfortable fit, etc.), but when I tried the Asics, my feet were finally happy! This year, I'm experimenting with a lighter type of shoe (Saucony ProGrid Kinvara 2), which I'm using for shorter runs (five to ten miles). I like the lightweight feel and the small heel, which helps me concentrate on maintaining a mid-foot strike.

Bra:

As important as getting the right pair of shoes for a comfortable and reduced-injury run is finding a bra that will provide proper support. Research has shown that sports bras provide this kind of support,[12] but it's up to you to find the specific one that fits you best. Sports bras tend to be made of wicking material, which encourages moisture to travel away from the skin, keeping you dryer. Staying dry is not only more comfortable, but also prevents chafing.

At my local running store, The Running Company, clothing experts help customers find proper running bras, just like footwear experts assist with finding appropriate shoes. Again, if you have no access to these kinds of running stores, most lingerie stores will have at least one knowledgeable employee who can take your measurements and help you find a good-fitting bra. If you'd prefer to take these measurements yourself, you can check out the online site, Bounce: (http://www.shopbounce.com/home.do).

The site suggests that you take these measurements while wearing your most supportive, non-padded bra. Also, you should reach "relaxed end expiration" while taking your chest circumference measurements. (That is, release the air from your lungs, but not forcefully.)[13] These measurements include:

- One inch below the armpit

- Full part of the breast

- One inch below the breast line

Once you've gotten your measurements, enter them into the "calculator," which will generate your bra size. The site also has "bra coaches" who will help you answer any questions you might have on how to find the perfect running bra.

A properly fitted athletic bra should cover the entire breast tissue, but there should be no extra fabric. Also, according to a Title Nine online bra coach (http://www.titlenine.com), it's a good idea to replace your bra as regularly as you replace your running shoes, so as not to lose support. She also advises owning two or more sports bras so you can use them on a rotating schedule and keep them lasting longer.

Clothing:

One of the most common complaints of runners is getting blisters, which are caused by friction force. To reduce the incidence of blisters on your feet, it's advised to use socks made out of synthetic fibers or wool. Moist skin increases friction force, and wool and synthetic fibers are not as absorbent as cotton. Socks that wrap around the arch of the foot are also recommended, because they keep their form and stay in place, thereby reducing the likelihood of extra fabric generating friction.[14, 15] These socks are on the expensive side, but they will last you longer and give you a more comfortable run. Some such socks are even designed anatomically for the left and right feet. In addition to enhancing the fit, this creates a minimal or nonexistent toe seam, thus diminishing toe irritation.

I have been very happy with the anatomically-shaped and seamless socks. For summer and road running, I like the "no show" socks that just cover your feet. For winter and trail running, I prefer socks that go up to your ankles. They're a little bit warmer and help keep rocks and debris out of my shoes on trails.

Like your socks and bra, synthetic fabric should be the choice of material for the rest of your running clothes, not only for the warm summer months, but the cold winter days as well. Synthetic textiles have wicking properties and retain less moisture than cotton, producing less shivering and sweating and allowing skin temperature to be restored to pre-exercise levels more swiftly.[16]

According to Jessie, a clothing expert at The Running Company, fabrics like wool and recycled polyester have natural wicking properties, while others have to be treated to acquire this property, which will eventually wash out. To make your running clothes last longer, carefully follow the washing instructions that come with them, and as soon as you feel they're not performing as well as they used to… well, it's time to go shopping again! Don't get me wrong; I'm not suggesting that you need to buy two or three new outfits before you start running, but following these clothing tips might make your start to running more bearable and worthwhile. There's nothing wrong with running in a cotton T-shirt, but you may experience improved comfort and results with a slightly more expensive shirt.

I personally like to wear tank tops and shorts in the summer, both made of wicking material. I prefer tank tops that have a small pocket in the back and a built-in bra. I rarely wear T-shirts on runs, and if I do, they are fitted and made of wicking material. I've also recently begun switching from baggier shorts to tighter ones. I don't like any extra fabric flopping around when I run. The less fabric I feel, the more comfortable I feel. The clothing brands I usually buy are Asics, Nike, Adidas, and Saucony, because I like the fabric these companies use. It feels soft, and it's cool in the summer and warm in the winter, without too much bulk.

During the colder months, I layer clothes according to the temperature. If it's around 40°F, I'll wear two layers: a summer tank top underneath and a fitted long sleeve shirt on top. When the temperature is lower, I add one more layer, and if it is windy, I might throw on a wind breaker. I wear gloves and hats made out of wool. They are soft and thin and keep me warm during the cold runs (45°F and below). I get most of my running clothes at running or sports stores or from the internet. For me, it's helpful to read reviews by other runners and try on some pieces.

Running Technique:

Running technique is very difficult to change, but if you are a beginner, you are in luck: forming fresh habits is much easier than breaking old ones! Recent research has revealed that running with a lower and fixed center of gravity and landing on the mid to front part of the foot will not only make you a more effective runner, but may also diminish your incidence of overuse and repetitive loading injuries.[17, 18]

What do I mean by running with a lower and fixed center of gravity? For most of us, our center of gravity is somewhere around the belly button. Keeping your spine and torso straight, if you lean forward a bit, your belly button will be a little lower than when you're standing perfectly upright. Running in this position will prompt you to step forward and land either flat-footed or with the mid sole, rather than the heel. If your center of gravity is up higher or back farther than your mid-section, indicating that you are leaning backward, you will tend to have a rear-foot strike. This is OK if you are walking, but when you add the landing impact of running, this type of strike can cause foot injuries.

And what does it mean to have a "fixed" center of gravity? This means you don't want to have too much bouncing in your step. (Picture your belly button steadily moving forward, with minimal up and down movement.) Bouncing while running adds impact and wastes energy. In addition, try to keep your hips from rocking side to side; you want to make yourself as streamlined as possible.

What about the stride? The length of your stride will depend on the strength of your push-off. If you have a strong push-off, then your stride will be long, and vice-versa. What is important here is where your feet land. If your feet are landing under your hip, then you are OK, regardless of the length of your stride. However, if your feet land in front of your hip, then you are over-striding. Over-striding will cause you to land on your heel, ahead of your center of gravity. In a sense, you will be braking with each step you take. If you want to run efficiently, concentrate on your push-off. A good push-off will propel  you forward and most likely, make you land on the mid to front part of your foot. (As you can see on the picture, try to extend the back leg all the way for a better push-off.)

So, to get into running position: stand up straight with your spine aligned; then (without breaking at the hip), lean forward until you feel like you have to take a step forward to avoid falling. In this position, you're ready to start running.

What to do with your arms? Keep them bent at ninety degrees and move them forward and backward to the rhythm of your pace, trying not to cross them in front of you. You can practice this while sitting on the floor, which will prevent you from overextending them. Open up your chest, lifting the rib cage: this will allow you to draw more oxygen into your lungs with each breath. Keep your shoulders down and relaxed to avoid unnecessary muscle tension. Same goes for the rest of your body: try to relax all your muscles except for the ones you need to run. During races, I always repeat to myself, "Relax your face, relax your face!" (I tend to grind my teeth when I'm concentrating.)

As far as your head goes, tuck in your chin, but keep your gaze elevated enough to see a few yards in front of you. This will allow you to check your terrain while keeping an eye out for anything approaching you.

Women-Specific Issues:

As women, we have at least three specific issues to worry about while running: pregnancy, breastfeeding, and personal safety. In regards to the first issue, pregnancy: can you run while pregnant? If you are a beginner, you may want to wait until the baby is born before taking up running. If you're already a runner, check with your physician. Most likely, you'll be able to keep on running, but you'll probably be advised to slow down a bit and reduce your weekly mileage. If you would like to start running after your baby is born, you can get started with a progressive walking program and add some strength training exercises. However, make sure you run it by your physician before you begin any training program. And don't forget to put a running stroller on your baby shower gift list!

If you are breastfeeding, you should again consult your physician and follow his or her advice closely. Personally, I had no problem with playing squash and field hockey and lifting weights while breastfeeding. I just had to make sure I was getting enough calories to accommodate the exercise and milk production. The most challenging aspect, for me, was finding the right bra! Luckily, nowadays, that's the easiest part. The last women-specific issue I'll discuss is personal safety. If you have to run very early in the morning or late in the afternoon, when it's dark or getting dark, make sure you are keeping your personal safety in mind. There are many strategies that you can implement to stay safe and still fit in that inconvenient run. The first strategy is safety in numbers; here we have another motive to recruit friends and/or family. It's always a good idea to run accompanied, but your company doesn't have to be running too; they can be alongside you in a car or on a bicycle! If you are running alone in a deserted area and wearing headphones, leave one ear free so you can stay aware of your surroundings. Try to always carry a cell phone with you and let others know when and where you are running. Map your runs, have an itinerary, and share it with friends or family. If you are in a new area because you just moved or you're on vacation, it's a good idea to ask around and check the web for running paths and/or groups in the area. When my family travels, we always ask at the hotel or the equipment rental shops about safe places to run. If we are in an urban area, we try to find parks or run through the city early in the morning, when traffic is the lowest. I love to do the latter; running is a great way to see and experience cities.

PAR-Q & You

Regular physical activity is fun and healthy, and increasingly more people are starting to become more active every day. Being more active is very safe for most people. However, some people should check with their doctor before they start becoming much more physically active.

If you are planning to become much more physically active than you are now, start by answering the seven questions in the box below. If you are between the ages of 15 and 69, the PAR-Q will tell you if you should check with your doctor before you start. If you are over 69 years of age, and you are not used to being very active, check with your doctor.

Common sense is your best guide when you answer these questions. Please read carefully and answer each one honestly: check YES or NO.

Yes	No	
		1- Has your doctor ever said that you have a heart condition and that you should only do physical activity recommended by your doctor?
		2- Do you feel pain in your chest when you do physical activity?
		3- In the past month, have you had chest pain when you were not doing physical activity?
		4- Do you lose your balance because of dizziness or do you ever lose consciousness?
		5- Do you have a bone or joint problem (e.g, back, knee or hip) that could be made worst by a change in your physical activity?
		6- Is your doctor currently prescribing drugs (e.g., water pills) for your blood pressure of heart condition?
		7- Do you know of any other reason why you should not do physical activity?

If you answered:

YES to one or more questions

Talk with your doctor by phone or in person BEFORE you start becoming much more physically active or BEFORE you have a fitness appraisal. Tell your doctor about the PAR-Q and which questions you answered YES.
• You may be able to do any activity you want — as long as you start slowly and build up gradually. Or, you may need to restrict your activities to those which are safe for you. Talk with your doctor about the kinds of activities you wish to participate in and follow his/her advice.
• Find out which community programs are safe and helpful for you.

NO to all questions

If you answered NO honestly to all PAR-Q questions, you can be reasonably sure that you can:
• start becoming much more physically active – begin slowly and build up gradually. This is the safest and easiest way to go.
• take part in a fitness appraisal – this is an excellent way to determine your basic fitness so that you can plan the best way for you to live actively. It is also highly recommended that you have your blood pressure evaluated. If your reading is over 144/94, talk with your doctor before you start becoming much more physically active.

DELAY BECOMING MUCH MORE ACTIVE:
• if you are not feeling well because of a temporary illness such as a cold or a fever – wait until you feel better; or
• if you are or may be pregnant – talk to your doctor before you start becoming more active.

PLEASE NOTE: If your health changes so that you then answer YES to any of the above questions, tell your fitness or health professional. Ask whether you should change your physical activity plan.

Ch 2

Run for Fun, 5 & 10 K

The first part of this chapter is for those of you who want to start a running program for any motivation other than completing a 5 or 10k. In the second part of the chapter, I will present a program for those of you whose goal is just to finish a 5 or 10k, and those of you who would like to increase your performance at either of these distances (your objective doesn't have to be completing a competitive race; it could be just you and the road/treadmill.)

Training Theory

Regardless of which program you chose to follow, from Run for Fun to a marathon, the training variables (frequency, intensity, and duration) and principles (overload, specificity, individuality, and hard/easy) used in this book will be the same. I will give you a quick review of these variables and principles, but if you want more information, you can find it in the Reference section at the end of the book.

Training Variables

Frequency: this variable refers to the number of days per week that you have to exercise (run, in this instance) in order for a program to have an impact on either your health or your fitness progress.

Intensity: refers to how hard you have to work for changes to occur in your system. If you are a beginner, moderate intensity will work for you; if you are more advanced, you will need to work harder to achieve results.

Duration: indicates how long the daily sessions should be to stimulate progress. A formerly sedentary person will benefit from as little as two bouts of 10 min a day of exercise, while a fit person will require at least 30 min a day to see changes.

These training variables go hand in hand with each other, especially duration and intensity. For example, if the exercise is vigorous, less time is needed to achieve results; conversely, if the intensity is moderate, your daily session is likely to be longer.

So how do we use these variables to make the exercise safe and progressive? Start with three days a week of running/walking (20 to 30 min). After four weeks of this, extend the sessions a bit – by 10%, to be precise (e.g., 22 to 33 min). Next, increase the frequency by adding one extra day of running/walking per week. Lastly, boost the intensity of your workouts. For example, if you are a beginner, one of your weekly sessions will consist of more running than walking. If you are already running the entire 30 min, you can increase your speed on certain days. We'll talk more about this later.

Training Principles

Using four basic training principles (overload, specificity, individuality, and hard/easy) will ensure that your exercise regime is safe and progressive.

Overload: refers to the stress applied to the system (i.e., your body). You have to overload your system to make it respond and adapt to the new demand. If you've never run before, just adding a few seconds of easy jogging to your usual walk will overload your system and stimulate it to accommodate the added stress. As you progress, those few seconds of jogging will have to become minutes in order to have the same impression on your system. If you are already a runner, your overload strategy will need to incorporate extra miles and/or harder workouts to produce positive adaptations.

Specificity: testifies that for maximum results, the training must be closely related to the event. In other words, if you are training for running, you must train with running. Moreover, if you are trying to achieve a certain distance, your training should be specific to that distance (e.g., long runs to prepare for a marathon or short sprints to get ready for a 5k).

Individuality: tells us about how exercise may have particularized results. If you and a friend are following the same exercise program, you may find that each of you reacts differently to the same stimulus. Individuality depends on your genes, the length of time you've been exercising, and your tolerance to exercise. We can't do anything about heredity, but fitness level and tolerance to exercise can each be developed.

Hard/Easy: this principle states that alternating hard and easy workouts will produce better adaptations to the stimulus. It works like this: if you have a hard session on Monday, then Tuesday should be an easy one, to let the body recover from the workout without losing a training day. Working hard all the time could lead to overtraining, which we will discuss more later.

In sum, to ensure that your training will be effective, you must apply the right overload, be specific to your running goals, consider your individuality, and alternate hard and easy workouts.

How to Monitor Intensity

If you have a heart rate monitor, checking the intensity of your workout is easy. If you don't have access to a heart rate monitor, don't worry; you can learn to keep track of your intensity without one.

There are a few methods of monitoring exercise intensity without fancy equipment. I'll introduce two that are easy to use: the "talk test" and the Borg Scale of Perceived Exertion. Just like it sounds, the talk test assesses your ability to talk during a workout:

- Low intensity: you can talk nonstop while exercising.
- Moderate intensity: you can sing the verse "Mary had a little lamb" without gasping for air.
- High intensity: you can't even think about talking!

During most of your runs, you want to be at a moderate intensity level. For the warm up and cool down, a lower intensity is OK. At the beginning of your training, you may feel that you are working at high intensity all the time. This may be true; just try to keep the exertion short when you are gasping for air. If you need to, return to a brisk walk. It's never easy to get started, but if you follow the program and pay attention to your intensity levels, you will be able to get into the groove without too much struggle. Let's face it: the beginning will be rough, and some days will be harder than others, but where there's a will, there's a way. Don't forget your big picture!

The Borg Scale of Perceived Exertion is another way to check your intensity if you don't own a heart rate monitor or are taking medications that affect the heart's response to exercise. The shaded areas are the ideal intensity to exercise.

Borg Scale of Perceived Exertion

Very, very light	6
Walking	7
Very light	8
Slow jog	9
Fairly light	10
Conversational pace	11
Moderate	12
Moderately hard	13-14
Hard	15
Breathing is deep	16
Very hard	17
Elaborated breathing	18
Very, very hard	19
Total exhaustion	20

Target Heart Rate

If you have a heart rate monitor, you will be able to see your heart rate while working out, but how does that translate to your intensity? To make sure you're hitting a good intensity, you should first find out your target heart rate (THR). This is the range of your heart rate in beats per minute (bpm) from low to high intensity. To ascertain your THR, you will need to check your resting heart rate (RHR) and your maximum heart rate (HR max). Your RHR is obtained by taking your pulse for one minute while at rest, either seated or lying down, during a calm period of your day. If you don't have a heart rate monitor, a good spot to find your pulse is your carotid artery (on the side of your neck). Just place your index and middle fingers softly against your neck, and as soon as you can feel your pulse, count the number of beats for a full minute. You can also find your pulse on your wrist, in that little groove under your thumb beside the finger's tendons. Turn one palm up and gently place your index and middle fingers on top of the radial artery. Never use your thumb to check your pulse, since the thumb has a pulse of its own and can confuse you. You can derive your HR max by subtracting your age from 220 (HR max = 220 - your age). Now that you have your RHR and your HR max, you can use the Karvonen formula to calculate your THR.

Karvonen Formula:

$$THR = (HR\ max - RHR) * (intensity\ in\ decimal\ form) + RHR$$

As an example, let's use this formula to find out the THR of a woman who is 47 years old and has a RHR of 75 bpm:

First let's find out her maximum heart rate:

HR max = (220 - age) → **HR max** = 220 - 47 → **HR max = 173 bpm**

Now let's fill in the formula with the numbers we know:

THR = (173 - 75) * (intensity in decimal form) + 75

The recommended intensity range for cardiorespiratory fitness is 60 to 80% of VO_2 max (maximum amount of oxygen that a person can utilize during intense or maximal exercise). If you are a beginner, you can go as low as 45-50% of VO_2 max and still benefit from the exercise. You may also find that having your HR upwards of 60% of VO_2 max feels like high intensity, and that's just fine for a beginner.

$$\text{THR} = 98 * (0.60 - 0.80) + 75$$
$$\text{THR min} = 98 * 0.60 + 75 = 134$$
$$\text{THR max} = 98 * 0.80 + 75 = 153$$

$$\boxed{\text{THR} = 134\text{-}153}$$

According to these calculations, our hypothetical woman should increase her pulse to 134 bpm when she is working at a low intensity and should not exceed 153 bpm by more than 3-5 beats when working at high intensity.

Now that you know all that, I hope you understand my schedules, so let's get ready to run!

Run for Fun

This program is for those of you who want to start running just to get moving. Even if you are currently sedentary with a 5 or 10k goal in mind, you can get started with this 8-week program. Afterwards, you can pick up the other two programs: 5 and 10k. And if you don't want to do the races, you can just follow the programs as a mode of progression. Starting with this program, you can easily build up to any desired distance and stay at whatever level suits your lifestyle and fitness goal.

I will start from the very bottom, so if you have been sitting around and not doing much lately, the first part of the program (Weeks i and ii) is for you. If you have been walking consistently or going to exercise classes, then you can get started later on in the program. The goal of this program is to get you to run continuously for 20 minutes at a time.

All workouts will follow the same order: warm up, main session, and cool down.

Warm up: the goal of the warm up is to get the blood flowing, loosen your joints, and prepare your body for the workout. In this program, the warm up is not incorporated into the schedule, so before you begin each workout, engage in a brisk walk for 5-10 minutes depending on how you feel that day, as well as how cold or hot it is and how hard you think the workout will be. (If it's too cold and the scheduled workout is a tough one, or if you're feeling a little under the weather, extend the warm up).

Main session: this is shown in minutes at the bottom of the table; the top letters (a, b, c, etc.) describe the type of workout to follow that day.

Cool down: do a nice slow walk for 3-5 minutes to help the body return to a pre-exercise state. During exercise, blood is directed to the working muscles and tends to pool in the legs when the exercise is over. Thus, if you stop abruptly, you might feel dizzy from lack of blood in your brain.

If you are short on time, make the main session shorter; never skip the warm up or cool down. Safety first!!!

Run for Fun, 8 Week Plus Training Schedule						
Weeks	M	T	W	Th	F	Sa	Su
i	20	30	off	25	off	25	35
ii	25	off	30	30	25	off	40
1	off	a 20	off	a 20	off	XT	b 25
2	b 22	off	a 22	off	c 28	off or XT	d 28
3	c 23	off	d 23	d 25	off	XT	e 30
4	d 23	off	e 25	off	e 27	off	f 27
5	e 25	off	f 17	off	f 23	off or XT	g 30
6	off	f 25	off	g 20	h 25	XT	h 33
7	off	g 25	off	i 25	j 25	XT	k 35
8	g 25	off	h 20	off	l 15	off	m 20

a: 1 min jog, 1.5 min fast walk, repeat 6 times
b: 1.5 min jog, 2 min fast walk, repeat 6-8 times
c: 2.5 min jog, 1 min fast walk, repeat 6-8 times
d: 3.5 min jog, 40 sec fast walk, repeat 6-8 times
e: 4 min jog, 30 sec fast walk, repeat 4-6 times
f: 6 min jog, 1.5 min fast walk, repeat 2-4 times
g: 5 min jog, 30 sec fast walk, repeat 3-5 times
h: 7 min jog, 1 min fast walk, repeat 2-4 times
i: 6 min jog, 20 sec fast walk, repeat 3-5 times
j: 8 min jog 40 sec fast walk, repeat 2 times
k: 10 min jog, 1 min fast walk, repeat once, 6 min jog, 30 sec walk, repeat once
l: 12 min jog
m: 20 min slow jog (slog) – no walking!!!
Off or XT: take the day off or cross train (engage in any kind of exercise with no impact, such as cycling, swimming, rowing, etc.)
XT: cross train (engage in any kind of exercise with no impact, see above)

5k, Beginner and Intermediate/Adv.

If you have been keeping active with any sport or aerobic exercise, you are certainly ready to start either program: beginner or intermediate. Just take a look at each and decide which one fits you best. The first program, as it's name suggests is for first timers, the second program is geared for those who have completed a 5k before and are looking for a better time and/or experience. In these programs, the warm up and cool down are included in the total duration of each workout, so you don't have to add time to these sessions, as with the Run for Fun program. The warm ups and cool downs should be done at a considerably slower pace than the main set (ideally, you will jog them, but if needed, you may walk briskly instead).

5k for Beginners						
Weeks	**M**	**T**	**W**	**Th**	**F**	**Sa**	**Su**
1	20	off	25	off	30	off	35
2	off	25	25	off	30	off	40
3	off	25	27	off	35	off	45
4	25	off	30	off	27	off	40
5	off	25	30	off	30	off or XT	45
6	33	off	35	off	off or XT	25	50
7	off	37	off	35	40	off or XT	45
8	30	off	30	off	15	off	5k

Off or XT: take the day off or cross train (engage any kind of exercise with no impact, such as cycling, swimming, rowing, etc.)

If you are following a strength training program, you can do so on your off days. Later on, as your fitness improves, you may be able to strength train on the same days that you are running. (Of course, there's no rush!)

5k for Intermediate/Adv. Runners						
Weeks	M	T	W	Th	F	Sa	Su
1	35	off	a 30	off	40	off	45
2	off	35	a + 1 35	off	45	off	50
3	35	off	a + 2 45	off	47	off	55
4	35	off	a 35	off	45	off	50
5	off	40	b 30	off	c 40	off or XT	55
6	40	off	b + 1 45	off	off or XT	c 38	60
7	off	45	b + 2 40	40	off	c + 1 30	45
8	c 40	off	b 35	off	20	off	5k

a: after a 8-10 min warm up, find a hill* and run up it for 30-45 sec, walk or slowly jog back down, repeat 4 times
b: after a 10 min warm up, run fast** (no sprinting!!) for 45 sec, jog easy or walk for 90 sec, repeat 4 times
c: after a warm up of 10 min, run at your 5k goal pace *** for 4 min, easy jog for the reminder of the time
Off or XT: take the day off or cross train (engage any kind of exercise with no impact, such as cycling, swimming, rowing, etc.)

As with the 5k for beginners, the warm up and cool down are included in the total time of the session, so start and end the workout slowly (you can read about warm up and cool down on the previous pages). The numbers at the bottom of the table represent the time in minutes you are expected to run that day, and the letters at the top of some of the cells describe the type of workout you can do that day. When you see a letter, a plus sign, and a 1 or 2, add either one or two repetitions to that drill. For example, on Wednesday of Week 7, it says "b + 2" and 40 minutes. This means that you will do a 10-min warm up, followed by 45-sec fast running, then 90 sec of slow jogging or walking. You will then repeat all of this 6 times (not 4, as it says under the description of the exercises).

10k for Beginners

This program is for those who have completed 5ks before and are looking to increase their distance. You can still follow this program if you've never done a 5k: just add Weeks 5 and 6, maybe even Week 7, of the 5k program for beginners to the start of the 10k program. This will add distance to your runs and pave the road for the more demanding program.

Warm up and cool down are incorporated into each workout session.

10k for Beginners							
Weeks	**M**	**T**	**W**	**Th**	**F**	**Sa**	**Su**
1	off	30	off	35	30	off or XT	45
2	33	off	38	off	33	off or XT	52
3	off	40	off	40	35	off	57
4	32	off	35	off	35	off or XT	53
5	off	35	40	off	35	off or XT	60
6	off	40	off	45	off	35	66
7	45	off	50	off	30	35	44
8	40	off	30	off	30	off	10k

Off or XT: take the day off or cross train (engage any kind of exercise with no impact, such as cycling, swimming, rowing, etc.)

10k for Intermediate/Advanced Runners

This program can be adapted for the advanced runner who wants to increase distance and intensity. If you are an intermediate runner, skip the runs under each x, and instead do any kind of aerobic exercise that is non-weight-bearing. This will give your joints time to recover while still challenging your aerobic system. Advanced runners: you can also switch to an alternate aerobic exercise on days that you wish you were on vacation.

Again, warm up and cool down are included in the duration of each workout. Unless otherwise noted, do 5-8-min slower-pace jog at the beginning and end of the workout.

10k for Intermediate/Adv. Runners							
Weeks	**M**	**T**	**W**	**Th**	**F**	**Sa**	**Su**
1	off	30	off	a 40	30	x 35	50
2	30	off	a + 1 45	off	40	x 30	55
3	30	45	off	a + 2 45	x 35	off	60
4	40	off	b 45	off	45	off or XT	55
5	off	30	c 40	off	x 30	40	65
6	off	40	c + 1 35	45	off	x 30	70
7	45	off	d 60	off	50	x 45	42
8	c 40	off	b 30	x 30	20	off	10k

a: after a 10-min warm up, find a hill* and run up it for 1 min, walk or slowly jog down, repeat 4 times
b: after a 10-min warm up, run fast** (no sprinting!!) for 1 min, jog easy for 1 min, repeat 4 times
c: after a 10-min warm up, run at a faster pace than usual for 3 min, easy jog for 1:30', repeat 2 times
d: after a 10-min warm up, run at your 10k goal pace *** for 10 min, easy jog for the reminder of the time
x: cross train if you haven't been running at least 5 times a week for at least 4 weeks before starting this program.
(cross train = bike, swim, row, or other non-weight-bearing exercise)

As with the 10k for beginners, the warm up and cool down are included in the total time of the session, so start and end the workout slowly (you can read about warm up and cool down on the previous pages). The numbers at the bottom of the table represent the time in minutes you are expected to run that day, and the letters at the top of some of the cells describe the type of workout you can do that day. When you see a letter, a plus sign, and a 1 or 2, that means add either one or two repetitions to that drill. For example, on Thursday of

Week 3, it says "a + 2" and 45 minutes. This means that you will do a 10-min warm up, followed by hill runs of 1 minute, with walking or slow jogging back down. You will then repeat this 6 times (not 4, as it says under the description of the exercises).

*Hill runs: these will help you build power in your legs. They are great for proper technique training. When you run up a hill, you will tend to lean forward and land on the mid or front part of the foot, which experts say is best for avoiding injuries. One thing to keep in mind, however: when you lean forward into the hill, make sure you're tilting your whole body, not just your torso. You don't want to break at the waist. When doing hill repeats, try to keep a consistent pace; don't slow down nor speed it up. Later on when you have many miles on your legs, you can do a descending hill repeat drill: the last repetition should be the fastest of all. For now, try to keep your regular pace (which can be challenging enough!)

**Fast run repeats: These will "wake up" your fast twitch muscle fibers (the ones used for sudden, fast movements). These runs should be considerably faster than your regular jogs, but not as fast as sprints. Leave the sprints for the pros, or take them up after a few years of running, to avoid injury. Try to do the fast runs in descending mode, so your first one is the slowest and your last one the fastest. This will teach you to pace yourself, too.

***Pace goal runs: If you have a time goal for your 5 or 10k, translate that time into minutes/mile – that will be your pace goal run (see Appendix for pace table). For example, if your goal is to finish your 5k in 30 min, you should be running 10-min mile (actually, just a bit faster, since a 5k is 3.1 miles). Practicing running at your pace goal (slightly under 10 min/mile) will give you an idea of what to expect on race day.

At the Races

If you are a beginner, you will be better off in a local race with as few participants as possible (although if you live in New York City, the smallest races in Central Park are in the thousands!) On race day, get there early enough to visit the port-a-johns, look around, and/or familiarize yourself with the procedures. If it's cold, bring a jacket and maybe an extra sweatshirt to change into after the race. The one you will be using during the race might get wet, and that will make you extra cold after the event. Most races have a parcel drop-off, so you can bring a small bag with the extra clothing and/or food (especially if they don't feed you after the race, which I doubt!).

Before the race starts, position yourself in the middle of the pack; this way, the fast runners don't have to weave around you, and you're not stuck behind the walkers in the back. Additionally, it always helps if you know the terrain of the course. If it's a flat route, then you won't have a problem. However, if you know there is some elevation, make sure you are prepared for it. Take the hills easy; even walk them up if you need to. You don't want to have to deal with oxygen deprivation before the end of the race! Familiarity with the terrain is another advantage of local races.

Race Strategies

A common beginner mistake is to start too fast. Your heart is pumping, you are anxious, and you see everybody around you going fast, so your tendency is to follow the crowd. Positioning yourself in the middle of the pack will help you regulate your pace. (Believe me; I have made the mistake of starting in the front!) That said, a 5k is a short and quick race, so you won't have much time to warm up during it. If it's your first one and all you care about is finishing, start slow and finish strong. Use the first mile as a warm up and think of the last two miles as your race. Set short-term goals, such as running to the stop sign or the lamp post or try to get passed the lady with the ponytail. Once you reach your short-term goal, you can even take a few walking steps before you resume running. Keep it light and entertaining: the race will go faster and be more fun. On the other hand, if you are looking for a good finish time, you should warm up before the race. You can get warmed up with a 5-8 min easy jog. If you are really going for your PR (personal record), you can add 5-6 short sprint repeats after the warm up (run 1/4 to 1/2 of a block fast, walk back, and repeat 4-5 times). The sprints will wake up your fast twitch fibers, and you will be ready to go when the gun fires.

A 10k will give you more time to warm up during the race, but it's also more important to pace yourself with longer races. A good rule of thumb is to run the first half at a slightly slower speed than the second half. Find your rhythm and keep your pace comfortable until the second half, but remember it's a race! After the first 5k, you can slowly start to increase your speed, by just a few seconds at a time. When you can see the finish line, run it out fast to the end. You'll look great, especially if you remember to smile for the cameras!

How Anna and Maureen Got Their Running Start

When Anna was in her mid forties, she and four other friends decided they needed to lose weight. They got together and each put a dollar in a jar, and they agreed that whoever lost the most weight would win the five dollars. As part of their weight loss plan, each friend kept a detailed log of what she ate and resolved to try to cut extra calories. The contest lasted five or six weeks. Anna is very competitive, but she didn't earn the five dollars. She shed a few pounds, but when she reviewed her food log and realized she couldn't really cut any more calories than she already had, she knew she had to start moving if she really wanted to get healthy and lose more weight. Thus, shortly after she lost the contest, Anna decided to start running. She didn't even consider joining a gym, because she knew it didn't fit her lifestyle and she wouldn't keep up with it. To her, running was the easier and more convenient solution.

Anna started her running program by running two blocks towards her friend's house, then walking back home. The next time she went out, she added one more block, then another, and so on, until she had reached a total running distance of three miles. After that, she stuck with three miles three times a week, but continued working towards longer distances during the weekends. Eventually, she got up to five miles. After she reached her weight goal (shedding a total of 25 pounds), she got a lot of compliments from friends and family, but she knew she had to stick to the running if she wanted to keep the weight off.

A year or so passed and Anna won my personal training services at a silent auction that we both attended. After the three complimentary sessions were over, she hired me as a trainer, and after I got to know her, I asked her if she might consider increasing her running distances or entering a few local races. Anna gave it a shot: she started running longer distances (first 10k, then half-marathons) and placing in her age group in local races.

Then, in 2004, I asked Anna if she wanted to try a marathon. She immediately told me that I was crazy. A few months later, she informed me that she had signed up for the Philadelphia marathon, and asked if I would train her for it. Since completing Philly, Anna has run at least one marathon a year. In 2007, she qualified for the Boston marathon, which she ran the following year. Boston marathon qualifiers must meet a certain time standard, depending on their age group. In Anna's case, she needed to complete a marathon in 4:05 hours or less. In 2009, Anna placed third in her age group in a regional half-marathon (Long Branch Half in NJ) and achieved her best marathon time in Chicago (3:41 hrs, positioning her 33rd in her age group).

Ten years after she began running, Anna kept off all the weight she lost. She not only got herself running, but she also motivated six of her friends and her whole family, (see pic below, Richie Jr. was overseas at the time) including her husband, Richie, and their three children, Richie Jr., Matt, and Stephanie, to start running (you will hear more about Steph later on).

You might think that Anna is a natural born athlete, but when I asked her about her previous exercise experience, I was pretty surprised to find that it was almost nonexistent. She had only worked out to Jane Fonda tapes after each of her kids was born, to help her lose the baby weight. So, how did Anna get to be where she is now? She says that she's very competitive and running worked out for her (she also tried tennis, but that didn't  turn out as well). According to Anna, when she finds something she likes, she works hard to become good at it, and enjoys pushing and challenging herself.

And what is Anna's motivation to keep running, now that she's lost the weight and achieved impressive times in long, difficult races? Her immediate response was, "Sheer vanity." She went on to explain, "When people tell me that I look great, I like to hear that. Those two words were never in a sentence with my name before I started running, and I like the sound of it. I do get the runner's high once in a while, and I like the feeling of accomplishment after a long run, but the truth is that I like how I look and how I feel now, and I enjoy the compliments." She added that she needs goals, or at least a schedule, to keep her running. She wants to know what she is doing next and run with a purpose, whether that be a race, recovery, or transition running.

Anna is not the typical kind of client I get; she is, in all honesty, an outlier. That said, I think anyone can draw some motivation and inspiration from her story.

Like Anna, the subject of my next success story, Maureen, didn't have an athletic background. Maureen's initial motivation to start running was the same as Anna's: to lose some weight. When she was in her mid-twenties, a friend of hers was running 5ks and five mile races, and this friend suggested to Maureen that she give it a try, too. Maureen did, and she immediately liked the atmosphere and the ongoing motivation to achieve a better time in each race. She established and met several short-term goals along the way, such as walking less every time, or finally running an entire race.

Maureen continued to challenge herself in times and distances, but she never felt satisfied with her times, and she never pushed herself to run more than five miles at a time. Then the kids came, and, with each of her pregnancies, more weight than she expected. Exercise then became her way to lose the baby weight and have some time for herself.

After her second child, Maureen decided to take on the challenge of a half marathon. After her third, she began training for a full marathon. Finding the time to do so was tricky with three small children, but with the help of her husband and her coach, Melanie Fink, she pulled it off and completed her first 26.2 mile race.

Before long, Maureen had finished six marathons with impressive times. Like Anna, she eventually qualified for Boston and ran it in 2010 in 3:42. One of Maureen's biggest continuing motivations to run is the opportunity to teach her kids about setting and following through with goals. In her own words, "I try and look at all aspects of life an opportunity to teach my kids, and setting goals, whether to run a marathon or qualify for Boston, is awesome for the kids to see. When I was working towards qualifying for Boston, I tried to make sure I got the most out of every workout, knowing that I would not have time to fit something else in."

According to Maureen, the key to achieving your running goals, or any other kinds of goals, is organization and planning ahead. As a woman yourself, with or without kids, you can probably relate to that!

In the picture, you can see Maureen with her family. Her kids are her number one fans (dad's too!)

Ch 3

Nutrition

A healthy diet can reduce the risk of major chronic illnesses, such as heart disease, diabetes, osteoporosis, and some cancers.[19] We have all heard this before, and yet the question I hear most frequently as a personal trainer is: What do I eat? My answer to that question is: eat mostly fresh, unprocessed foods, all types of vegetables and fruits, whole grains, lean proteins, and healthy fats, including nuts and seeds. When I tell clients this, they usually look at me as if I'm talking in code. I guess in a way I am, so let's carefully decode my advice:

1. Eat fresh, unprocessed food: Highly processed foods are those that come in packages and have a really long list of ingredients, many of which will be hard to pronounce. Most fresh food is not packaged and thus easy to spot. When purchasing packaged food, even if it claims to be "natural" or "healthy," make sure that you carefully read the labels. Some packaged foods, like meat substitutes, are supposedly healthier alternatives to raw foods like pork or beef, but be wary when their list of ingredients is long, complicated and seemingly written in a foreign language. Same thing goes for breakfast cereals that claim to be extra nutritious and natural: unless the cereal is steel cut oatmeal or looks anything like the original grain (don't get me started with colorful cereal), it's processed. Most prepared meals also fall into the category of processed food.

The risk of having a diet comprised of mostly processed foods is that even if everything you eat is low in fat or cholesterol, added sugar and sodium ends up being high and hard to control. If you prepare your meals from scratch, you can adjust the amounts and sometimes the kinds of fats, sodium and sugars that you put in.

According to the 2010 Dietary Guidelines,[19] the daily sodium intake for healthy adults and children should be less than 2,300 milligrams (mg), the calories from saturated fatty acids should be less than 10 percent (which can be achieved by replacing them with monounsaturated and polyunsaturated fatty acids), and the total daily amount of dietary cholesterol should stay below 300 mg. The guidelines also call for limiting the amount of calories that come from added sugars and solid fats, and restricting consumption of trans fatty acids, or synthetic sources of trans fats, such as partially hydrogenated oils. It's also recommended to reduce "consumption of foods that contain refined grains, especially refined grain foods that include solid fats, added sugars, and sodium."

All of this can be easily achieved by eating fresh, unprocessed foods. At the end of this chapter, I will present a few recipes for nutritious meals packed with fresh ingredients, which can be prepared in little time. You don't have to limit your diet to raw carrots and celery in order to follow this advice; there are many ways to prepare delicious foods without all the extra processed ingredients or the added sodium, fats and sugars.

2. Eat all types of vegetables and fruits: if you broaden your range of fresh produce, you will not only increase your intake of nutrients, such as folate, magnesium, potassium, dietary fiber, and vitamins,[19] but you'll add variety to your diet and have more cooking options. If the only vegetables you can think of are potatoes and corn, then that's all you will be compelled to cook with.[20] Same goes for fruits; there are way more out there than apples and bananas!

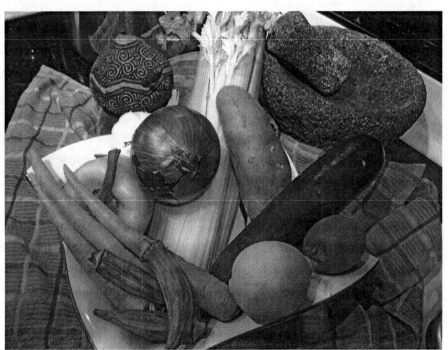

Some vegetables and fruits, such as leafy greens (kale, collard greens, chard, etc.) and berries, have been linked to reduced risk of certain cancers, including lung cancer. In a recent study, scientists found that the increment of as little as 100 g of produce a day (roughly one large orange), was associated with a lower risk of lung cancer (6-15% of some cancers).[21]

Nowadays, you can find a great variety of "exotic" veggies and fruits in most supermarkets. For most people, the issue is what to do with them, and how to incorporate them into the daily diet. A great way to get started is to visit your local farmer's market, or, if there is one in your area, join a Community Supported Agriculture group (CSA, http://www.localharvest.org/csa/). Either will provide you with access to local, seasonal food directly from the producers.

A few years ago, I joined a CSA in my town. I really enjoyed the experience, especially because it introduced me to vegetables that I had never tasted or heard of before, such as kohlrabi, now one of my favorites. It was a nice way to learn and practice cooking with new ingredients. My CSA had a newsletter that provided recipes and interesting information about the not-so-familiar veggies and fruits.

Nowadays, I mostly visit a couple of local farmer's markets and stop at my favorite vendors, which also offer recipes for the veggies or fruits in season. When December rolls around, I really miss my visits to the farmer's markets, and can't wait until June. In the meantime, supermarket veggies and fruits will do.

3. Eat whole grains: What's wrong with white flour, white rice and pasta? They come from whole grains too, right? Yes, they do, but they fall into the category of processed foods, which we talked about earlier.

Let's focus on flour, for example. White flour comes from wheat, which is a whole grain. The problem is that for the flour to reach the "white" category, it has to go through a process that strips it of most vitamins and minerals, which are essential for good nutrition. The wheat grain (or any kind of grain made into flour) has to be milled and then refined – processes which remove most of the fiber-rich bran and germ that contain valuable vitamins and minerals.

So what is wrong with "white" grain? Nothing, technically. In my experience, cooking with white flour, rice and pasta is easier than the whole grain counterparts. The bread comes out fluffier, the rice cooks faster, and the pasta tastes way better than whole wheat pasta. However, whole grains are a source of nutrients such as iron, magnesium, selenium, B vitamins, and dietary fiber, so why not make the change for health? It's a matter of priorities, but for me, the switch to whole grains is definitely worth it. Even though manufacturers add some minerals and vitamins back to refined flours, they're never restored to their original levels.[19]

Thanks to the various kitchen gadgets available today, cooking with whole grain doesn't have to be a challenge. I use steel cut oatmeal for breakfast, make my own bread using whole wheat, and when I make rice, I only use brown rice, even for risotto. And it's not very hard, thanks to the internet and slow and pressure cookers.

Now, with pasta, I haven't made the crossover into healthy whole grain yet. I don't eat pasta very often, so when I do, I make it with white flour, because I really don't like the texture of the whole wheat pasta. Who knows, maybe someday I'll be fully motivated to make the transition.

4. Eat lean proteins: These include legumes, too – not only poultry and meats. That's the beauty of the legumes; they can be counted as veggies and lean proteins! What are legumes, you might ask? Think of beans, peas and lentils. (Oh my!) Besides being a great source of proteins, legumes contain soluble and insoluble fibers, are low in fat (and the fats they contain are beneficial), free of cholesterol, and high in folate, potassium, iron and magnesium.[22] The dried form are a little bit more time consuming to prepare than the canned variety, but if you are worried about sodium, you might want to extend the extra effort. Or, if you go with black eyed peas or lentils, these don't require prior soaking.

Tofu, made from soybeans, is another lean protein alternative if you don't want to eat meat. I make meatless meatloaf (I know it sounds silly, but it is delicious!) using veggies, beans and tofu. With the right amount of spices and herbs, it comes out great: even my meat-lover husband likes it.

Now let's discuss lean proteins that come from animal sources: they contain 2-3 g of fat and 55 calories per serving, according to the National Heart Lung and Blood Institute, part of the National Institutes of Health.[23] (One serving = 1 oz of either skinless chicken or turkey, salmon, or lean beef – the one with no white streaks and the peripheral fat trimmed).

I know that the fat in beef meat and the skin on poultry are what make them tasty, but they also make them unhealthy. But the truth is you don't have to settle for dry, flavorless meats. Using herbs, spices, and low sodium broth, you will be able to enjoy great-tasting meat that is also good for your body. It might take a bit more time and effort in the beginning, but just like running, once you get the knack of it, it will become effortless and, who knows, before long, enjoyable!

5. Eat healthy fats: Fat is not limited to Jack Sprat's wife; we all need to eat it! Healthy fat, that is. Fat is the most important way to store energy in the body, functioning as a thermal regulator and a cushion for the internal organs. Fat allows us to ride horses and jet skis and motorcycles and run (wink, wink ☺) without worry of bruising any important organs. Some essential nutrients are only soluble in fat, such as Vitamins A and E, and the essential fatty acids that come from fats serve as the raw material for important molecules in the body. Last but not least, fats are an important part of every one of our cells' outer layer, or cell membrane.

Some essential fatty acids, such as linoleic and linolenic, which are part of the groups called omega-6 and omega-3, respectively, play important roles in the composition and development of the cerebral cortex and the retinas, and are intimately involved in the proper functioning of the heart and immune system.[24] Without fats, our cells would have defective membranes, we couldn't process essential vitamins such as Vitamin A, which would make us all blind, and without thermal protection and cushioning, we would be super cold or super hot in most weather. Moreover, our internal organs would be bouncing all over, making it really hard for us to do anything, and especially run. The moral of that story is: eat your healthy fats!

Now that I've convinced you that fats are good for you, let's try to sort out which are the "healthy" ones. In general, vegetable oils contain polyunsaturated and/or monounsaturated fat. Both of these are desired in a healthy diet. The two best types of vegetable oil commonly found in US stores are canola oil and olive oil. In fact, it's been suggested that the latter may lower the risk of heart disease.[24, 25]

However, some vegetable oils, even though they are liquid at room temperature, contain saturated fats and should be avoided. These include coconut and palm oil. Saturated oils are usually used in highly processed foods, which is another reason to avoid these kinds of foods. Additionally, manufacturers sometimes alter the fats and fatty acids in processed foods to keep them fresh longer and change their characteristic appearance (i.e., turn solid fats into liquids using a method called hydrogenation). Saturated fats and trans-fatty acids, present in butter and lard, are solid at room temperature and have been linked to cardiovascular disease.[24] Therefore, these fats should be avoided whenever possible.

Make sure you read the labels on the foods you buy; if you see the word hydrogenated in the ingredients or if the amount of saturated fat per serving is 20% of the daily value (DV) or higher, then it's wise to find an alternative (the healthiest items will be either low in saturated fat, which is 15% of the DV, or free of it).[26]

Another good source of healthy fats as well as protein are nuts and seeds. Consumption of nuts is associated with a lower risk of heart disease and diabetes.[27] Additionally, some nuts and seeds, such as almonds and sunflower seeds, are high in Vitamin E (peanuts and cashews are not).

Eating fresh nuts and seeds will ensure a higher intake of Vitamin E, just like with other foods. Olives, also high in Vitamin E, lose their concentration of this vitamin when they are processed to become olive oil. One study found that up to 90% of the Vitamin E in olive oil degrades after 12 months of home storage. A final reason to eat fresh foods, in this case nuts and seeds, is that some studies have found possible adverse effects of taking Vitamin E supplements.[28, 29]

Despite all this, a large percentage of the U.S. adult population does not consume nuts or seeds (except for peanuts). Nuts and seeds may be packed with nutrients, but they are also high in calories, so they should be consumed in limited portions. Nuts and seeds make a great mid-morning/afternoon snack and are a great addition to salads and vegetable dishes (just make sure that you buy the raw kind to ensure that they are not loaded with extra oils and/or salt).

I buy raw nuts and seeds and toast them in batches using the toaster oven or taking advantage of leftover heat from the conventional oven. Then I put them in glass jars and store them in the fridge. I usually always have pine nuts, cashews, almonds, walnuts, sesame seeds, sunflower seeds, and pumpkins seeds on hand, and I use them every day, either as snacks or in meals.

You've probably figured out that I'm not a big fan of prepared or processed foods, but if you have to buy them, reading the nutrition labels is a must. Several studies have demonstrated that the well informed consumer who places importance in nutrition also practices a healthful lifestyle. However, you must be wary of tricky nutrition and health claims.[30, 31, 32]

Most nutritional marketing is found on products designed for children, but many others target health-conscious adults with catchphrases like "all natural" and "good source of fiber." Unfortunately, almost half of the processed foods that claim to be "low in fat," "a good source of calcium," and "made with whole grains," are high in saturated fat, added sugars and/or sodium. Be wise: don't stop at the claims; read all the ingredients. If you stay informed, you will make much better and healthier choices.

In the next page, you will find a table with the recommended daily servings per food group for a diet between 1800 and 2000 calories, according to the 2010 Dietary Guidelines.[19] I added some input on the serving sizes to give you an idea of what constitutes a serving. Using a food scale will give you an even better idea, since going by volume is not as accurate as weight, especially for all the different kinds of breakfast cereals out there. Some are denser than others, so the food scale will provide a more accurate picture. Measuring out serving sizes might sound a little obsessive, but you shouldn't have to do it for long. As soon as you get familiar with what constitutes an ounce of this or that, you can stop weighing out everything you put in your mouth.

Recommended Daily Servings

Food group	Servings	Serving size
Grains	**6** (preferable 3 of them from whole grains)	1 oz: 1 slice of bread; in cereal, 1 oz will depend on the kind of cereal- it could be as much as 1 ¼ cup or as little as ½ a cup. ½ cup cooked pasta, rice or other grains
Lean meats, poultry and fish	**6** or less	1 oz cooked meats or 1 egg. One medium pork chop, half of a small chicken breast and/or a small hamburger will constitute roughly half of the daily servings, with an average weight of 3 oz
Vegetables	**4-5**	1 serving equals 1 cup of raw leafy vegetables, ½ cup of veggie juice, or ½ cup of chopped, raw or cooked vegetables
Fruits	**4-5**	1 medium fruit, ½ cup of fresh, chopped fruit (also canned or frozen), ¼ cup dried fruit, and ½ cup fruit juice (please, please, home squeezed!!)
Dairy (low fat or fat free!!)	**2-3**	1 cup milk or yogurt or 1.5 oz of cheese
Max sodium intake	**2300 mg**	
Oils and fats	**2-3**	1 tsp vegetable oil. Mayonnaise (1 Tbsp), margarine (1 tsp) and salad dressing (1 Tbsp) are listed here too, but try to avoid them
Legumes, nuts and seeds	**4-5** per week	½ cup cooked legumes (beans or peas), ⅓ cup nuts (the amount that you can hold in a cupped palm), 2 Tbsp peanut butter or seeds
Sweets	**5 or less** per week	1 Tbsp sugar or jelly, ½ cup sherbet, 1 cup lemonade (homemade, please!!)

I started eating much healthier about six years ago, after my youngest son became a vegetarian. Preparing one meatless dish at meals made me start eating less meat, too. I became what is known as a "pastatarian." I ate meat once a week and the rest was mostly starches. The problem was that I was participating in long distance races (between four and six hours in length), and my body didn't appreciate the change. I started feeling weak and my performance took a nose-drive. When I saw my physician for an annual check-up, she told me that I was anemic. She advised me to alter my diet and take a multivitamin daily to increase the amount of hemoglobin and ferritin in my system.

Around that same time, I came across a recipe book ("You are What You Eat," by Dr. Gillian McKeith) that uses mostly vegetables and legumes as ingredients, and I took to it. Dr. McKeith incorporates a lot different veggies, legumes and beans, as well as a variety of fruits, and she flavors her dishes with spices and herbs instead of relying solely on salt.

When I first started following her recipes, I became very frustrated because I didn't have most of the ingredients she called for. But my frustration didn't last long. One day, my daughter and I made a list of the most frequently used ingredients in the book, and the amounts we'd need to make a week's worth of breakfasts, lunches and dinners, including mid-morning and mid-afternoon snacks and healthy desserts. The list was long and it took us a couple of days to gather all the ingredients, but we succeeded.

The moral of the story is to have the ingredients at home. If you have a selection of healthy ingredients and recipes, you'll be forced to come up with healthy meals. Additionally, healthy recipes do not have to be complicated, hard to follow, bland, or tasteless. Nowadays, there are many healthy cookbooks out there; even Alton Brown has one! Even though I never ate fast food and almost always prepared my meals at home, it took me a couple of days to get used to the new tastes of Dr. McKeith's recipes. She uses many spices with which I had little to no experience, such as turmeric and coriander seeds, and in only a few recipes does she call for salt.

After my daughter and I had created a week's worth of menus with our healthy ingredients, we wrote out another week's worth. When we had repeated each of our recipes once, we started improvising using primarily the ingredients in the book. We have been cooking this way ever since, and everyone in the family loves it. Although I don't eat perfectly all the time, I would say that I do about 80% of the time, and I'm very happy doing so. Sometimes I fall off the wagon, but the next day I get back on track, and everything is good again.

As I promised earlier, I will provide a few recipes that I use to incorporate whole grains, fruits, veggies, nuts and seeds, and vegetable oil in my diet. Your meals don't have to be flavorless to constitute a healthy diet. If you are used to eating processed food, you might have to retrain your taste buds a bit to appreciate simple flavors. Fortunately, this doesn't take long. The first two or three times you try these new recipes, you might find them bland, but as you move away from highly processed foods and into the fresh type, you will learn to taste the "real" flavors of the ingredients. Before you know it, you'll consider most prepared and processed foods too sweet or salty, and that's a good thing (as Martha would say).

Breakfast favorites:

For winter (W): Overnight steel cut oatmeal with dried fruits, nuts and seeds
For summer (S): Fresh fruit with almonds or fresh fruit smoothies

Lunch favorites:

W: Veggie soups (many kinds)
S: Big salad

Snack favorites:

Nuts and dried fruits

Dinner favorites:

W: Shiitake mushrooms risotto
S: Quinoa and veggie salad

Recipes

1. Overnight steel cut oatmeal with dried fruits and nuts and seeds

This recipe is my version of Alton Brown's "Overnight Oatmeal."[33]

You need a slow cooker for this recipe, but the beauty of it is that you'll have a warm bowl of delicious breakfast cereal waiting for you as soon as you get up in the morning!

Ingredients: (4-5 servings)

1 cup steel cut oatmeal

4 cups water (or rice milk)

1 ½ cups dried fruits, nuts, and seeds mix (match to your taste: e.g., raisins, dates, dried figs, cranberries,* dried cherries, walnuts, cashews, pecans, crushed** flax seeds, sunflower seeds, etc.)

Directions:

Mix everything in the slow cooker at night before you go to sleep (8 hours at least), set it on low, and get ready for a delicious breakfast first thing in the morning! You can add a tablespoon or two of low fat or fat free yogurt to your meal. I like to have this kind of breakfast when I know I will have a long morning, because it keeps me full for hours.

* These have added sugar, so be careful about how many you use.

** Buy the flax seeds whole and crush only the amount you will use; the oil that is released when the seeds are crushed loses its nutrients quickly. (I use an old, clean coffee grinder for this).

2. Fresh fruit with almonds

Ingredients: (2 servings)

1 banana

1 kiwi

1 orange

2 Tbsp sliced almonds home roasted

2 tsp oat bran

Directions:

Mash the banana and divide in two bowls, cut the kiwi in small pieces and divide into 2 bowls. Press the orange and divide into bowls, and also add 1 Tbsp of almonds and 1 tsp of oat bran into each bowl. Combine and Presto!

I love this as breakfast or snacks during the day. Sometimes, if I'm really hungry, I will have the whole 2 servings at once.

3. Vegetable soup

In this case, use whatever you have in the house. I will present my favorites, but you can replace the veggies with whichever ones you have available. My recipe makes a pretty sweet soup, so I don't make it when my younger son is visiting from college.

Ingredients: (4 servings)

1 butternut squash*

1 sweet potato

4-6 collard greens leaves

2 carrots

2-3 onions

1 clove of garlic

1 Tbsp of low sodium vegetable broth

A bunch of parsley or cilantro (washed)

* You can save the squash's seeds, toast them in a toaster oven for 4 min or in the oven for ~10 min, and add them at the end with the cilantro, mmm!

Wash thoroughly and cut all the veggies into cubes (if they are organic, I don't peel them), and save the parsley for the end. Place them in a pot or pressure cooker, cover with water (about 3-4 cups), add the vegetable broth, and simmer. Cook for about 20-25 minutes (in a regular pot), or 10-12 minutes in a pressure cooker after the pressure valve goes off. If the veggie pieces are small enough to fit in a spoon, you can leave as is, or you can use a hand blender and cream the soup. Last step is to chop the parsley or cilantro and add it to the soup, and you're ready to dig in!

4. Big Salad

(You probably don't need a recipe for a big salad, but I will tell you how I make mine)

Ingredients:

A bunch of baby greens,

1 shredded carrot,

½ bell pepper (red, yellow or orange),

2-3 baby bella mushrooms,

parsley or cilantro chopped,

3-4 cherry tomatoes,

1 stick of celery chopped, and

1 tsp each of cashew nuts, dried cranberries, and any kind of seeds (sunflower, crushed flax seeds, pumpkin seeds, or sesame seeds).

Dressing:

1 Tbsp of olive oil,

1 Tbsp of mustard, and

1 ½ tsp vinegar (balsamic, apple, or grapefruit – which I recently tried and is delicious!).

Mix it well; it becomes an emulsion, which is better for coating each ingredient of my big salad (not Elaine's).

5. Shiitake mushroom risotto

Ingredients: (4 servings)

3.5 oz shiitake mushrooms, clean, with out the stems

1 ½ cups of brown rice, any kind (short grain is better, but what ever you have will do)

1 ½ tsp low sodium vegetable broth (or ½ cube of regular sodium vegetable broth)

2 ½ cups water

Directions:

Place all the ingredients in a slow cooker set to low and cook for 4-5 hours. You can replace the mushrooms with any type of vegetable. If you forgot to set up the slow cooker and need prepare dinner in a hurry (under 30 min), you can do a faster version of this recipe using a pressure cooker. Add the same ingredients to the pressure cooker and when the valve goes off, lower the temperature and let it cook for 20 min. When I make the fast version, I usually use butternut or acorn squash instead of mushrooms (the mushroom risotto takes a bit more preparation, and I tend to have squash in the house more often than mushrooms.)

6. Quinoa and veggie salad

Ingredients: (4 servings)

1 cup quinoa, cold, previously cooked (prepare it as you would white rice)

1 carrot, shredded

2 small beets, previously cooked* and diced

1 bell pepper, cut into thin slices

1 can of artichoke hearts, cut into quarters (drained)

1 small head of Romaine lettuce, washed, drained and chopped

2 celery stalks, chopped (replace with fennel if available/preferable)

A handful of cherry tomatoes

¼ cup olives (pitted)

2 Tbsp toasted pine nuts

3 oz feta cheese

Dressing:

1 Tbsp olive oil,

1 Tbsp mustard

1 tsp vinegar, any kind (organic apple cider vinegar will do)

1 tsp lemon juice

Mix well, make into an emulsion

Directions:

Mix all ingredients; add parsley, mint, or chopped cilantro if you like. You can replace the quinoa with brown rice, lentils, beans,** millet, or any other kind of legumes or whole grains that have been previously cooked. Quinoa and beans are high in protein (14 g and 9.6 g per 100 g serving, respectively), but you are more than welcome to use chicken or fish, such as tuna, to make it into a whole meal.

* Place the well-washed beets in a semi-covered bowl with water and microwave for 8-10 minutes. Be careful: when they are done, they are extremely hot. After cooling, cut the beets into bite-sized pieces.

** Gas-free soak: To eliminate the indigestible sugars that cause gas, cook the beans for 2-3 min in boiling water (use 10 or more cups of water for 1 lb of beans), then cover and let sit overnight. Rinse the beans and cook them according to the recipe directions the next day.

Bon Appetite!

3:59.34
Ch 4

Marathon
Training,
Half and Full

This chapter will focus on half marathon and marathon training, covering assorted aspects, from reading a training schedule to finding your way into a big race. If you are preparing for either a half marathon or a marathon, the first step is to clearly define your overall goal, as well as some short-term goals to help you achieve your main objective. Running with a goal in mind makes training much easier, especially during long runs or extreme weather conditions.

On some occasions, you might find yourself wondering, Why I am doing this to myself? What is the point? Keeping your short and long-term goals in mind will help you tough it through these low points. Remind yourself of the progress you have made towards your goal, and refocus your attention on what you must accomplish that day to stay on track. If you are a beginner, your main goal will most likely be to finish the race. If you are a long distance race veteran, your main goal will vary, from improving your personal best time to qualifying for a more selective race.

Regardless of what your overall goal is, never lose sight of it while training! Training with a purpose is the best way to keep yourself better motivated.

In this chapter you will find:

- Training schedules for half and full marathons, for both beginners and intermediate/advanced runners
- What to do when training days are lost (sickness, travel, obligations, etc.)
- Specific training vocabulary (for intermediate/advanced schedules)
- How to choose a race
- Nutrition: pre-race, race day, and post-race
- Race day strategies
- Marathon training and family life considerations

How to read training schedules

These schedules follow the training principles of periodization. Periodization is a training method that uses fluctuations in the variables (running time and distance) to systematically adjust the total work load of the exercise. This method encourages continually improved performance and averts both premature plateau and injury. The key to periodization lies in periodically giving the muscles adequate time to rest, so they can keep adapting to increases in stress.

The numbers you will see in each of the schedules represent minutes, except on Sundays, for which the longer runs are posted in miles. The idea behind training schedules is to accomplish the time or the distance on Sundays, walking as little or as much as you need. In all the training schedules, the running volume increases by 10% each week, with the exception of Recovery Week. Recovery Week is indicated by a downward-pointing arrow in the "Weeks" column. These recovery weeks are the rest periods of the training, following the principle of periodization.

You will also notice letters on top of some running days. These indicate different types of workouts. An **x** above a weekday means that if running five days a week is too much for your body, you can switch to a no-impact aerobic activity, such as swimming or biking, on that particular day. This will give your joints a break while continuing to challenge your aerobic system. On some occasions, you might need to take that day off completely and that is OK; listen to your body.

Starting on Week 7 in the beginner's schedule, you will see a (t) on top of Friday runs. The **t** stands for "terrain." If your race has some elevation but you're training on mostly flat terrain, you might want to find a hilly area to practice in on (t) days. (If you live in FL, look for bridges and go up and down, up and down). However, if you usually train on hills or your race is flat, then you can ignore the (t)'s in the schedule. If you are following the intermediate/advanced  schedules, the (t)'s will be replaced by "Hills." In the intermediate/advanced schedules, you will also notice the terms "Pace," "Tempo," and "Speed."

Definitions for these vocabulary can be found between the half and full marathon training schedules.

Additionally, in both schedules you will see a (d). These appear on Sundays of Weeks 8 and 9 for the half, and Weeks 14 and 15 on the full. The (d) stands for dress rehearsal. On these days, you can try running in the outfit you plan to wear on race day. If you are going to use new shoes for the race, you can try them out during Taper Week. This will give you the opportunity to see if they feel OK, yet keep them in almost new condition for the race. You'll see that Taper Week is also the week of the race. During that week, the training volume is decreased by about 50% from the previous week; however, the intensity is the same. This kind of taper will reduce fatigue and increase your performance during race day.[34]

What to do with training days lost? If you miss one to four training days, just skip those days and stick to the schedule. You don't need to make up for a few lost days. However, if you miss five to seven days of training, return to the schedule for another full week. For example, if you miss your Thursday morning run because you overslept and you have a birthday party that night, just skip that workout and pick up with the next scheduled run.

On the other hand, if you completely missed Week 3 of the schedule, maybe because of an illness or a trip, resume at the beginning of Week 3. This will set you back a bit, but it's important to resist your impulse to catch up with the schedule. Increasing your total volume or jumping too quickly into the long runs will lead to overexertion and a decline in immune system performance. As a consequence, you could get sick (or sicker if that's why you lost the week) or injured, and you are much better off going into a race undertrained than stuffed up with a cold or limping!

Half Marathon Training

The half marathon is one of my favorite distances. It is challenging enough to make you work hard, but it doesn't leave you worn out after training or even race day. That said, a half marathon will be much more enjoyable if you train for it properly (remember that I'm writing from experience too!)

The only long run I did when preparing for my first half marathon was nine miles, and I'm telling you, that was not enough! Was I ever sore after the race!! But, lesson learned; now I not only run at least 11 miles while training for a half, but I do more than one long run. Thorough training might take more time and effort, but it makes long races much smoother, and you'll feel much better when you're done.

Wondering how long it will take you to finish a half marathon? Here's a little statistic: out of approximately 7,000 women who competed in the More Magazine/Fitness Magazine Women's Half Marathon in NY in 2011, 50% finished the race between 1:50 and 2:20 hrs.[35] This is a reasonable time if you are fit and have been running for some time, but if you are a complete novice, knocking off a half marathon might take you three hours or more. This doesn't mean that you won't enjoy the experience; as long as you are having a good time and are in good company, the race will go by faster than you would imagine.

In the next pages, you will find two half marathon training schedules: one for beginners and another for intermediate/advanced runners who would like to improve their half marathon times or are accustomed to long distances but have not entered a half marathon race before.

Beginner Half Marathon Schedule

11-Week Half Marathon Schedule for Beginners (Remember that Sunday runs are in miles!)							
Weeks	M	T	W	Th	F	Sa	Su
1	off	40	off	45	30	off or XT	5
2	40	off	45	off	33	off or XT	6
3	off	45	off	50	35	off	7
4	30	off	45	off	40	off or XT	6
5	off	45	50	off	40	off or XT	7
6	30	40	off	50	off	25	9
7	45	off	50	off	(t) 40	30	10
8	30	off	50	off	(t) 45	30	(d) 9
9	off	45	50	off	(t) 30	35	(d) 11
10	off	45	50	off	(t) 30	35	6.5
Taper 11	45	off	40	off	30	off	**race**

Off or XT (cross train): take the day off or engage in any kind of exercise with no impact, such as cycling, swimming, rowing, etc.

(t): Terrain. Train for hills if the race will have them and you're used to running on flat surfaces.

(d): Dress rehearsal. Wear what you plan to wear for the race on these long runs.

Tip for the long runs: It is OK to walk as much as you need to in order to finish the distance stipulated. You may also take short breaks to catch your breath and resume running or walk/running when you feel capable. If you're still worried that the long runs will be too stressful on your body, you can split them into two mid-sized run/walks, one in the morning and the other in the afternoon. Doing it all together will prepare you better for race day, though!

Intermediate/Advanced Half Marathon Schedule

Due to the introduction of speed workouts and longer and more frequent long runs, it is important to have accumulated miles to take full advantage of the intermediate/advanced schedule.

11-Week Half Marathon Schedule-Intermediate/Advanced						
(Remember that Sunday runs are in miles!)						
Weeks	**M**	**T**	**W**	**Th**	**F**	**Sa**	**Su**
1	off	40	off	45	40	x 30	6
2	40	off	45	off	35	x 30	8
3	off	45	off	50	35	x 30	9
4 ↓	30	off	45	off	40	x 35	7
5	off	H 45	50	off	40	x 35	8
6	x 35	50	off	P 55	off	40	10
7	45	off	H 60	off	50	x 30	12
8 ↓	40	off	T 55	off	50	x 30	(d) 9
9	off	S 45	60	off	45	x 35	(d) 12
10	30	off	P 60	off	x 45	35	6.5
Taper 11	S 40	35	x 30	off	15	off	**race**

x: Cross train (bike, swim, row, or other non-weight-bearing exercise) if you haven't been running 5 times a week for at least 4 weeks before starting this program, or if running 5 x a week is too much.

H: Hills. Do a 10-15-min warm up, then jog up a hill for approx. 40 sec, repeating 3-6 times. Easy jog the rest of the time with a 5-min cool down.

P: Pace. Warm up for 10-15 min, then run between 30 and 40 min at your anticipated half marathon pace. Cool down 5-10 min.

T: Tempo. Warm up for 15 min, then run at a slightly faster speed than your anticipated half marathon pace for 20-30 min Cool down 10 min.

(d): Dress rehearsal. Wear what you plan to wear for the race on these long runs.

S: Speed. Warm up for 15 min, then run fast for 50 yards or 45 sec, followed by a jog/walk or easy run for 100 yards or 1 min Repeat 4-10 times. Cool down 5-10 min.

S (T): Speed for Taper Week. Warm up 15 min, then do 4 repetitions of 50 yards (or 45 sec) of fast running to 100 yards (or 1 min) of easy jogging/walking. Easy jog the rest of the time with a 5-min cool down.

Specific Training Vocabulary

For veteran runners with many miles accumulated, adjusting your speed during training will make your running more efficient and eventually improve your race time. Incorporating speed work and hills will spice up your training, making the sessions seem shorter. The times laid out in the following workouts are a guide. Don't fret if you did it five to ten sec faster or slower, but you may need to reevaluate your fitness level if you're missing the times by a min or more.

Hills: This workout will improve the power in your legs by recruiting more muscle fibers. Boost yourself up the hills by leaning your whole body forward; do not break at the hips. Keep your stride shorter and more frequent, but try to stick to your normal pace. Start with a good warm up, and then do a few repetitions of the hill, each time walking or jogging easily back down. Attempt the next hill when your breathing has calmed down and you feel that you will be able to finish it in the same time or a few seconds faster than the previous run. Start with 4-5 repetitions and add one or two more in the next scheduled **H** workout.

Pace: This workout will help you get accustomed to your anticipated race pace. Warm up for 10-15 min and then run the designated time at your anticipated race pace. This might feel slow on a short run, but it is important that you know how it feels to run at the pace you will be sticking to for most of the race.

Tempo: Run slightly faster than your pace run. These workouts are a bit shorter than pace workouts because they are more intense. The faster pace will challenge your aerobic system so that the next time you run at a slower speed, it will feel easy, making you more comfortable during your long runs.

Speed: These are the last workouts in the schedule because they are the most intense of all. The purpose of speed workouts is to recruit fast twitch muscle fibers, the ones needed to eventually increase your overall speed. Do a prolonged warm up before this workout so your muscles and tendons are ready for the high intensity exercise. These workouts are best done on a flat surface. Do 4-5 repetitions of the designated time or distance, depending which race you are training for. Each rep should be slightly faster than the previous one, but try to keep your speed under control. Do not sprint; this is much too fast and may lead to injury. Try to keep your maximum speed around the pace of your best 5k race.

How to Pick a Race

Flat or hilly? Big or small? Co-ed or women only? Well, all of this will depend on your local options. However, as far as terrain goes, try to pick a course that has a similar topography to what you're used to training on, especially if it's your first race. If you're training on mostly flat terrain, try to avoid races with lots of hills; your legs will thank you in the end.

As for the size of the race, that's up to your personal preference and availability. Smaller races will be more low-key and may be a better fit for someone who's just looking to finish the race. On the other hand, a big race (10,000-40,000 plus participants) might be a good motivator for someone who appreciates cheering crowds and social support. In a small race, it will be easy to find your way to and from the parking lot, gear check, port-a-potties, and starting line. However, in a big race, all these logistics will have to be sorted out beforehand; you don't want to be running around, stressed and exhausted, before the race even begins.

In either case (small or big race) you will most likely need to pick up your race materials a day or two before the race. Even so, you'll probably want to arrive a good two hours early on the big day. One thing to consider with big races is public transportation or parking (remember, another 9,999 to 39,999 people will be looking for parking spaces at the same time!) So leave yourself plenty of time to get there and park. After that, you'll have to find your way to the baggage facility, stand in line to use the port-a-potties, find your starting wave, and finally stand in place for 15 to 20 minutes until the gun goes off (hopefully it won't be super cold or super hot for this!)

Of course, when you're finally finished racing, exhausted, and ready to collapse at home, you'll have to get back in line to pick up your bag, use the port-a-potties, and find your car/your way back home. Another issue to consider with the big races is that they usually have a time limit (about three hours for a half and six to seven for a full marathon). Oh, and I almost forgot to mention the best part about these big races: most starting times are seven a.m.!!! I'm not trying to scare anyone off of big races; they are always a lot of fun. However, they do require a bit more planning and preparation, so just make sure you've thought through all the details before the big day.

Another option for races is the "women only" type. These are great for ladies who might feel more comfortable running among other females in their first race. There are many organizations that host these types of races: Lady Speed Stick has many half marathons in various locations (womenshalfmarathon. com), and More Magazine hosts a women's half marathon in New York. Additionally, Nike sponsors women's half and full marathons in San Francisco. Hopefully there will be one near you if you're interested.

My first half was a small race in a farming community, and my first marathon was in New York City. It was a big race back then, and it is an even bigger one now! While I have enjoyed small, local races, I personally prefer big races in big cities. There is always a lot to see, and running is a great way to give yourself a thorough city tour.

Marathon Training

You may be wondering, How long will it take me to finish the marathon? As with half marathons, this will depend on your fitness level, but here's another statistic: out of the approximately 4000 women who participated in the 2011 Nike women's 26.2 race, 50% finished between 4:30 and 5:30 hrs.[36]

The infamous 26.2-miler is a big fish to catch, but with proper motivation, the right amount of training and social support, you can do this! Oh, and I forgot one other thing: your doctor's permission. I would advise you, regardless of your age or conviction that you are fit enough for a marathon, to let your doctor know your intentions to run such a distance and follow his/her directions with care.

According to Ellen Seuffert, R.N., F.N.P, from Westfield Family Practice in NJ, "First-time athletes interested in marathons should have a physical exam with their primary care provider prior to begin training. This is no time to be cavalier." She urges athletes to get a medical clearance to discard any heart function anomaly, such as a slight heart murmur, or a mild irregularity, which can be aggravated if not properly monitored.

In the next pages, I present two schedules, one for beginners and one for intermediate/advanced runners. Remember that both of them are guides; you might need to make some adjustments depending on your initial fitness level, work/family obligations, weather, and potential illness/injuries, although let's hope you won't have to deal with the latter!

The first variable, initial fitness level, will determine which of the two schedules suits you best. The second variable, work/family obligations will influence how much time you can dedicate to training. Marathon training requires long runs that may take you 3 hours or more depending on your speed. Not only will you have to set aside time to complete these runs, but you'll need some more time to recuperate from them. Especially if you are a beginner, the ten plus mile runs can really wear you out. Even if your next day is filled with work, soccer games, antique shopping, and heavy thinking and decision making, you'll likely have to fit in a few cat naps!

The next variable, weather, can also affect your training, especially the long runs. Cold, rain, snow, humidity, and/or heat will probably be unavoidable at some point, regardless of your location. On some occasions, you may need to find an indoors alternative, shorten the run, or split it into two sessions.

As for the final variables, illness/injuries, while we never plan for them, they do happen. Unfortunately, at some point during the four plus months that you are training, there is a good possibility you'll get sick or injured. If this happens, you will probably have to alter the training schedule by skipping some sessions or modifying them to accommodate the situation.

We will talk more about marathon training and each one of these variables later on, so if and when you think any of them may be an issue, you can give that section a read in the *What if...* chapter.

Marathon Schedule: Beginners

If this is your first marathon, this schedule is for you. However, if your initial fitness level is low, meaning that you have been sedentary or inactive for a long time, then you might want to tack on an additional four to six weeks to this 17-week schedule. I know 20 plus weeks sounds like a long time, but it will pay off in the end by sparing you from injury and fatigue and helping you cross that finish line.

Beginner Marathon Schedule

17-Week Marathon Schedule for Beginners (Remember that Sunday runs are in miles!)							
Weeks	M	T	W	Th	F	Sa	Su
1	off	40	off	45	30	off or XT	8
2	40	off	45	off	40	off or XT	8
3	off	45	off	50	40	off	9
4 ↓	30	off	50	off	45	off or XT	8
5	off	40	50	off	45	off or XT	9
6	25	40	off	50	off	x 30	10
7	40	off	50	off	x 35	30	12
8 ↓	off	35	45	off	x 40	30	10
9	40	off	50	off	40	x 30	12
10	off	45	55	off	x 40	30	14
11	x 40	off	60	off	(t) 50	35	16
12 ↓	off	x 35	50	off	(t) 45	30	15
13	30	off	55	off	(t) 50	x 35	17
14	off	35	60	off	(t) 50	x 35	(d) 19/F
15	off	40	55	off	(t) 65	x 45	(d) 20
16 ↓	30	off	50	off	x 45	(t) 35	12
Taper 17	45	40	off	30	15	off	**race**

Off or XT (cross train): take the day off or engage in any kind of exercise with no impact, such as cycling, swimming, rowing, etc.

x: Cross train (non-weight-bearing exercise, such as biking swimming, etc.) if running 5 times a week is too much.

(t): Terrain. Train for hills if the race will have them and you're used to running on flat surfaces.

(d): Dress rehearsal. Wear what you plan to wear for the race on these long runs.

Tip for the long runs: It is OK to walk as much as you need to in order to finish the distance stipulated. You may also take short breaks to catch your breath, and resume running or walk/running when you feel capable. If you're still worried that the long runs will be too stressful on your body, you can split them into two mid-size run/walks, one in the morning the other in the afternoon. Don't forget to bring a GU and/or sports drinks on these runs; they'll give you an energy boost when you need it. For the longer runs (1 ½ - 2 hrs. and above), and when it's hot, I bring a bottle with sports drinks and one gel for every 7 miles I run. My route has water fountains, so I take the GU right before I reach one, then I take a good gulp of water to help with the digestion of the gel. I also take a sip of sports drinks every 3 miles, up to when I take the gel. But this is me, you have to try what works for you. See more information in the coming pages, under nutrition.

19/F: Run 19 miles or engage in continuous aerobic activity, which can be a combination of running, walking, hiking, and/or bike riding (this one the least amount of time) for the duration it will take you to complete the marathon (in your best guess). This will get you used to enduring physical exertion for 4-6 hours nonstop.

Marathon Schedule: Intermediate/Adv. Runners

The following schedule is for returning marathoners who have run a minimum of 20 miles a week for the past five to six weeks and want to improve their Personal Record.

Intermediate/Advanced Marathon Schedule

17-Week Marathon Schedule-Intermediate/Advanced						
(Remember that Sunday runs are in miles!)						
Weeks	**M**	**T**	**W**	**Th**	**F**	**Sa**	**Su**
1	off	45	off	45	45	off or XT	9
2	35	off	40	off	45	30	10
3	off	45	off	50	40	35	11
4 ↓	35	off	50	off	40	30	10
5	off	35	55	off	x 40	35	11
6	35	45	off	55	off	x 35	13
7	45	off	H 60	off	x 40	35	15
8 ↓	off	x 35	H 55	off	45	35	13
9	45	off	P 55	off	45	x 35	15
10	off	T 45	60	off	x 45	40	17
11	45	off	P 65	off	55	x 40	19
12 ↓	off	x 40	55	off	S 50	35	18
13	45	off	P 65	off	55	x 40	19
14	off	T 50	70	off	60	x 45	(d) 20
15	off	x 55	H 70	off	65	45	(d) 21
16 ↓	30	off	P 50	off	x 45	35	11
Taper 17	S (T) 45	P (T) 40	off	30	15	off	**race**

- **H:** Hills. Do a 10-15 minute warm up, then jog up a hill for 40 sec to 1 min, repeating 3-6 times. Easy jog the rest of the time with a 5-min cool down.
- **P:** Pace. Warm up for 10-15 min, then run 30-40 min at your anticipated marathon pace. Cool down 5-10 min.
- **T:** Tempo. Warm up for 15 min, then run at a slightly faster pace than your anticipated marathon pace for 20-30 min Cool down 10 min.
- **S:** Speed. Warm up for 15 min, then run fast for 100 yards or 1 min, followed by jog/walk or easy run for 200 yards or 2 min. Repeat 4-10 times. Cool down 5-10 min.
- **S (T):** Speed for Taper Week. Warm up 15 min, then do 4 repetitions of 50 yards (or 45 sec) of fast running followed by 100 yards (or 1 min) of easy jogging/walking. Easy jog the rest of the time with a 5 min cool down.
- **P (T):** Pace for Taper Week. Warm up for 15 min, then run at anticipated marathon pace for 15-20 min. Cool down for the remainder of the session.

Nutrition

Pre-race

You've surely heard of the expression "carbo-loading," but what does this term mean? Exactly when should you carbo-load when preparing for a half or full marathon? Carbo-loading refers to the increased ingestion of carbohydrates before a race for improved performance. Research shows that if done right, carbo-loading increases muscle storage of glycogen, the preferred muscle fuel for endurance exercise.

There are different methods of increasing glycogen stores in the muscle; however, eating a diet rich in carbohydrates for one to three days before the competition will do the trick. Make sure that you increase your carbohydrate intake and not your total calories (so watch out for those heavy sauces on your pasta!)

If the competition is longer than 90 minutes, carbo-loading will have a positive impact on your performance.[37] This is the time to indulge in all the white stuff I bashed in the nutrition chapter: white pasta, white rice, and potatoes. These foods are rich in simple carbohydrates, the type with high glycemic index. Glycemic index refers to the rate at which carbohydrates become present in the bloodstream and available for the body to use as energy. Carbohydrates with a low glycemic index will take longer to become available in the blood, while those with a high glycemic index will be more readily available for utilization by the muscles.

At the same time that you're loading up on carbs, you should decrease your consumption of dairy, excessive amounts of fruits and vegetables, and gas-producing foods like beans. These foods have a low glycemic index and can produce discomfort during exercise. Avoiding them for at least 72 hours before your race competition should help.

Race Day

Continuing the carbo-loading, choose high glycemic foods for breakfast on race day, such as toasted white bread with honey, peanut butter or jam. If you habitually drink coffee in the morning, you can also do so on race day. Moderate amounts of caffeine (no more than three cups) won't cause dehydration.[38]

Try to consume about two cups (16 oz) of fluid two hours before the race. This is a good time span to promote absorption of the needed fluids and excretion of the leftovers. It's also a good idea to pack a snack for the trip or for when you are waiting in line for the race to begin, as research has shown that consuming a snack less than one hour before physical competition improves performance.

If you have low blood sugar, you're best off eating something rich in carbohydrates five to fifteen minutes before exercising, or consuming a low-glycemic-index snack less than one hour before the competition.[37]

During the Race

Research shows that consuming carbohydrates during exercise lasting as little as one hour may also improve performance. You can consume these carbs in the form of sports drinks and/or solid foods or gels. To enhance absorption, the best combination of sugars is glucose and sucrose or glucose and fructose–

mixtures which are commonly found in commercial sports drinks and gels. These commercial products also contain electrolytes, which support muscle function, among other things, and are easily lost during heavy sweating.

The recommended amount of carbs for optimal absorption and performance in females is around 60 g of carbohydrates per hour. This can be attained by consuming one gel and half a cup (4 oz) of sports drink per hour. [37] Therefore, if you're going to be racing for more than an hour, it's wise to bring a gel or two along with you for the race.

There goes all my advice about processed foods, right? While you can bring a piece of fruit for the pre-race snack, I find gels much easier to take with me on a race. Likewise, highly processed sports drinks are probably better than fruit juice because they contain electrolytes.

If you don't like the idea or taste of sports drinks, you can consume electrolyte capsules or tablets and rely on gels for the carbs. Electrolyte capsules and tablets provide only the minerals needed to replenish those lost through perspiration. The tablets can be flavored, such as Nuun and GU brands; however, the capsules are tasteless. Hammer Nutrition sells both capsules and tablets, called Endurolytes and Endurolytes Fizz, unflavored. But if you don't mind sports drinks, you can find out what brand will be offered during the race

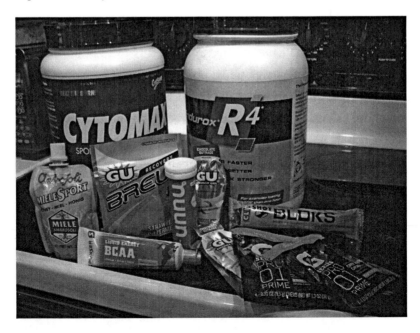

(Gatorade, PowerBar, HEED, etc.) and start using it during your long runs.

Now, if you don't like the taste of sports drinks at the beginning, give them a chance. A study has shown that the flavor of different sports drinks change for the best during exercise.[39] If a specific brand doesn't work well for you, or you prefer a different one, you can always bring a bottle of your own stuff with you to the race. Then you can alternate between your sports drink and water offered at the fluid stations.

It's also wise to experiment with gels before the race; if you plan on carrying one or two with you as you run, ask around and see what kinds other runners like and why. Most often, if not always, half marathon races do not offer gels during the race, so you will have to bring your own. Usually, marathon races will have a fuel station by Mile 18, but this is a long way for the average runner, who completes the 26.2 in four to five hours. For this reason, I bring my own gels, and my favorite brand is GU–chocolate and espresso flavors. Depending on how far I had to travel and how long it's been since breakfast, I'll have a GU gel or chomps (these have the consistency of Gummy Bears and have the carbs and electrolytes same as the gel) 15 min before the race starts, followed by a gulp of water. I usually bring a disposable water bottle to the race with me so I can have a few sips during the trip and after my pre-race snack.

How to Refuel

Congratulations; you have finished your race! Now to refuel your system! Your body needs two types of refueling: physical and mental. The physical should start right after you cross the finish line. Just as pre-race nutrition is important for enhanced performance, post-race nutrition is essential for a swift recovery. Timing and type of fuel play central roles in the rate of absorption.

The best way to refuel after a race is to consume fluids that contain carbohydrates and electrolytes, which most sports drinks provide. In this way, you can re-hydrate and refuel at the same time. Small amounts over short periods of time (i.e., 15-30 minutes) seem to be most beneficial right after exercise. Sipping about eight ounces of your favorite sports drink every 15 minutes with a solid snack, such as pretzels, will do the trick.

Replenishing your system is most critical for 30 to 60 minutes after exercise.[37] There are commercial recovery drinks that work very well too.

They have a combination of carbohydrates and a little bit of protein, which is essential for muscle repair after a race or a strenuous workout.

I bring a reusable water bottle with just the recovery powder inside, and after the race, I add water, shake it up, and sip it while walking back to my car or to taking the train back home. If you decide to do this, don't mix the powder with water beforehand, because the proteins will denature by the time you consume it. The recovery mix I'm using right now is called Endurox, and as you might guess by now, my favorite flavor is chocolate. You can find many kinds of recovery drinks and a variety of flavors; try some out during your training to make sure they work for you.

Once you've replenished your body, the mental refueling can begin. Take a few days to reflect on the whole your experience: start by applauding yourself for having participated in the race, then review your race goals and your training log (hopefully you kept one), and finally look back on the big day. Taking everything into consideration, decide if it you were able to get out of it what you were hoping to. Are there areas that need improvement? Are you are happy with how you did? You may be like me initially: after my first marathon, I said, "No more." But a few days later, I changed my mind, and here I am, many marathons later. If you find yourself feeling like I did, I hope you eventually change your mind, too!

Racing Strategies

We've already talked about finding your way to the starting line and pre-race fueling strategies. Now it's time to talk about what to do when the gun goes off!

Some races organize the participants in starting waves, posting minute/mile pace signs along the starting line so runners can place themselves according to their projected race pace. In others, participants are given a specifically colored bib, depending on their race history and/or the projected pace or finish time they indicated when signing up.

If there are no pace signs or waves, place yourself about mid-way through the pack. This is a good spot to start if you plan on finishing between 1:50 and 2:30 hours for a half marathon, or between 4 and 5 hrs for a full. If you think you may need longer, keep walking to the back of the line. There's no shame in that; it will only make your life and those of your fellow runners easier.

OK, now that you are well positioned, let's talk about race strategies. The gun just went off, and you are all excited, and the crowd is cheering, and start running fast! Well… let's not do that. These are long races, so you need to pace yourself. It's best to start slow, even when people are passing you left and right.

Think of the first miles as your warm up, and then fall into your desired pace. I had good results when I did the first half of a marathon slower (in just a few seconds per mile) than the second half. The trick is to curb your excitement at the beginning. Just take it easy for the first half. After that, you should be feeling really good, and you can pick up the pace a bit for the second half. The best part of this strategy is that you end up passing quite a lot of runners at the end of the race (some of which may have passed you in the beginning).

An alternate strategy is to stick to the same pace for the entire race. This actually is the best one, but it is harder to accomplish than the strategy of starting slow and finishing strong, especially if you are a beginner and if the race has hills (it's hard not to slow down going uphill, and you may not necessarily catch up on your way back down).

If this is your first long distance race, either a half or a full marathon, thinking of the total distance might be overwhelming for you. A good way to overcome this is to divide the race in sections that seem more manageable. These sections can be a mile, three miles, or up to the next light post, for all I'm concerned. Use whatever method works for you.

I like to use the fluid stations as markers, and I count them down during the race. One fluid station down, three to go, etc. I talk to myself quite a bit during races, mostly in my head, but sometimes even out loud. But call me crazy; it works for me!

Another way to mentally handle the mileage is to set the distance of your longest training run as your first goal. If your longest training run was 10 miles for a half or 20 for a full marathon, you should know what to expect up until you hit those mile markers. Then, after you've knocked off over three quarters of the race, you'll only have 3.1 or 6.2 miles to go. After all your training, those distances should be a piece of cake ☺.

To keep an eye on your pace, you can use your own stop watch or the digital clocks usually provided at the mile markers. Your time may be off by a few seconds or minutes, depending on where you started and the size of the race. But if you know when you crossed the starting line, you can do the math every time you see the clocks on the mile markers. You can also bring a GPS and set it to give you information mile by mile. Your Smartphone will certainly have an app for that too (check out the Gadget Chapter for more info). Gadgets are fun, but you really don't need anything fancy. You'll be fine if you rely on the digital clocks most races provide (the only trick there is to do the math and run at the same time!)

If this is your first long distance race, my biggest advice is just to go out and have fun. Hopefully, you will have some company for the race, which I highly recommend. Time goes by way faster if you have somebody to talk to, and you can keep each other motivated and on task.

Marathon Training and Family Life

Training for a long distance event takes a lot of patience and effort, but you and your family will have an easier time if you involve them in your training routine. Also, consider that your family will enjoy many indirect "perks" of your participation in these races, one of them of course being your health. The benefits you and your family will derive from your training will help to offset any strains between family life and marathon life.

As you saw in the training schedules, you will have to dedicate approximately four hours a week and another three to four hours on weekends at the peak of your training season. This commitment will have an impact in your daily routine, especially if you have young kids. Of course, by planning ahead and sharing responsibilities with other members of your family, you should be able to compensate for the time spent training.

A recent study[40] on amateur marathon runners reported that a sample of endurance athletes and their families employed many strategies to balance training and family life. One of these strategies was to include the family in their runs. Some ran with a family member, adapting their pace to include the companion; others had their kids or partners bike along with them during the runs. Good communication was found to be the key ingredient in maintaining harmony between training and family life.

Additionally, most of the non-running family members in the study reported that they benefited from the runner's training. One of the benefits they cited was interesting vacation destinations. Some runners like to race in different cities and/or countries, and often, they bring a family member or the whole family along.[40] Another indirect yet important benefit that running will bring to your family is improved mental health and mood. Marathon training is best accomplished outdoors, and spending time outside has many benefits, such as reducing work stress.[41] And remember: endurance exercise increases the release of endorphins – those "feel good" hormones that will lift your spirits and melt your troubles away.

I can provide several personal anecdotes on how balancing family life, work, and training can be accomplished smoothly and effectively. I've interviewed many women with young children who ran while their kids were at school. I've also spoken to some women who worked as teachers and picked fall races in order to take advantage of the summer break for training. As Jody Bohrman put it, "When I ran my marathons, I was a teacher in the Pocono Mountains, so my hardest running would take place in late spring, summer, and early fall. It was a huge bonus to have the option to sleep in or nap after my hard runs."

Based on my personal interviews as well as the research mentioned above, the most popular methods of balancing family, work and training for a marathon include: waking up early to run while family members are still asleep, running at times that won't affect family members, including family members in your training, and self-limitation, which is a compromise Anna Rowe made when she noticed her running affecting her family's balance. Anna and her family settled on a reasonable number of races for her to complete during a year, and her family's balance was restored.

I've personally seen many instances where the partners or older children of runners get inspired to pick up running themselves. Such was the case with Jody's husband and daughter, Anna Rowe's husband, son and daughter, and my own husband and daughter. In some cases, the relative will accompany the runner on outings; in other cases, they each venture out on their own.

Either way, participating in the same activity provides something healthy and motivational for family members to share. You can read the story of Anna Rowe's daughter, Stephanie, at the end of this chapter.

After all this talk of good communication and motivation among family members, you may be wondering if these strategies ever fail. Well, yes, involving family positively in your training experience doesn't always work out. A very funny example of this is one of my Monday strength training class participants, Laura Napolitano. One Sunday morning in November of 1995, Laura asked her husband to drop her off by the Verrazano Bridge on Staten Island, NY. When her husband asked her what she was going to do there, she had to snap at him, "Run the New York City Marathon!" Luckily, Laura's story has a happy ending: she still runs and loves to encourage her family to do so. Her daughters run 5ks with her and even her husband, who is more of a cyclist and swimmer, runs a 5m race with her every year. And when Laura ran the NYC marathon for the second time in 2008, she made sure to let her family know what she was training for! In the picture you can see Laura and her running companion Maureen ready to tackle the 2008 NYC marathon.

How Stephanie Got Her Running Start

"There are a lot of reasons that I started, and continue, to run. I started to run the summer before my freshman year of college. A big motivation for running was that I didn't want to gain that dreaded 'freshman 15.' More importantly, I started running because of my parents. They were already huge runners, doing marathons and running for hours every weekend. I knew that I was going to school 600 miles away from home, and I started running that summer so that I could spend more time with them. At first, I could barely breathe when I was running, let alone hold a conversation, but it gradually got easier and easier to talk and run at the same time. Even now, when I am home on school breaks, I go for a run with my parents to catch up and spend time together.

As I started upping my mileage, I got the idea in my head that I could try a marathon. My parents have been doing them for years, and I figured that I could try one myself. I already had two built-in marathon gurus to ask a billion questions. I was supposed to run my first with my mom, but had to postpone due to a foot injury. After I was healed, I started the training all over again, this time with a new running partner: my boyfriend. Three and a half months later we did it. We completed our first marathon in October, 2011 and we didn't die! Mission accomplished!!!

I have learned to love that feeling after a run. Some people call it 'the runner's high' and some call it crazy, but it is something I have begun to crave. I know that when I get back from a morning run, that I am going to have a great day. I will get everything done on my To Do List, and I feel accomplished because I've already worked out! Now I start to get antsy when I don't run for a few days. I feel that itch and find myself planning a run for the next possible free moment.

Right now, the biggest reason I run is because I am stressed. Some of my friends ask me how I can go for a run when I have so much on my plate already, and I always give them the same response: running is planned relaxation time. I know that if I go for an hour long run, I will only be able to put one foot in front of the other for the next hour. That's it. Nothing more, nothing less. As the run goes on, I feel myself relax and get into my rhythm. I forget about everything that is on my mind and I simply enjoy the time that I have to myself."

Steph, having a great time at a half marathon race

Extra Race Tips

Before the race:

- Have a good night sleep
- Stay well hydrated

At the race:

- Do not wear anything new
- Eat and drink at regular intervals
- Run at your own pace

At this time, the only thing you can change is your attitude, so:

SMILE FOR THE CAMERAS!!!!!!

Ch 5

Strength Training

Strength training is a valuable tool not only to improve running performance for beginners and veterans alike, but also to achieve and maintain general fitness and well-being. If you are an inexperienced runner, strength training will allow your body to engage more muscle fibers in running, making exercise feel easier. If you are a veteran runner, strength training will improve your performance by fine tuning those muscle fibers to do their work more efficiently. Most importantly, increased muscle mass and strength have been linked to many health benefits, such as reduced incidence of metabolic syndrome (people who suffer from this syndrome have high blood pressure, high blood glucose and large waist circumference), improved body composition, and increased bone mass and bone strength in areas where the stress was produced. And let's not forget those nicely toned arms and legs that you will get from strength training!

The ACSM[42] recommendations for adults seeking general muscular fitness with associated health benefits are as follows:

Resistance Training

- *Frequency:* train all major muscle groups (chest, back, arms, legs, core) 2–3 days a week.
- *Intensity:* (1) very light to light intensity may be beneficial for improving strength in sedentary persons beginning a resistance training program; (2) moderate to hard intensity for novice to intermediate exercisers to improve strength; (3) hard to very hard intensity for experienced strength trainers to improve strength.
- *Type:* a variety of exercise equipment (free weights, resistance bands/machines) and/or body weight can be used to perform exercises for each major muscle group.
- *Repetitions:* 8–12 repetitions are recommended to improve strength and power in most adults.
- *Sets:* a single set of resistance exercise can be effective if you are a novice exerciser. However, for most adults, 2 to 4 sets are recommended to improve strength and power.

- *Rest Intervals:* rest 48 hours between sessions.
- *Progression:* progress gradually, increasing first resistance, then repetitions per set, and finally frequency.
- *Sequence of Exercises:* large muscle groups (chest) should precede smaller groups (arms); multi-joint exercises (squats) should precede single-joint exercises (biceps), and higher intensity exercises should precede lower intensity exercises.

Adding corrective exercises and flexibility training to your routine will make it into a comprehensive muscular fitness program. Corrective exercises are used to stretch the stronger muscles and strengthen the weakest ones in order to restore balance in the joints. Additionally, including stretching exercises will help prevent injury. As Ellen Seuffert, R.N., F.N.P, from Westfield Family Practice in NJ says, even though "recent studies suggest that stretching is overrated, I think it is imperative for those of us over 40 (especially if we are in sedentary jobs by day) to stretch prior and after exercise."

In a study on muscular balance and core stability by Fredericson and Moore (as cited in Maschi & Williams),[43] the weakest muscles for most runners are: the gluteus, the muscles found in the front and side of the lower leg (shin muscles and peroneals), and the vastus medialis (the medially-located muscle of the quadriceps). However, the full list of commonly tight muscles is a bit longer, comprising the antagonist muscles of those listed above: hip flexors, calf muscles, and hamstrings, among others.

General Strength Training Routine

In the next page, you will find a general muscular fitness schedule. This routine is progressive, so it can be used by both beginners and experienced exercisers.

Warm up for 10-15 min by means of any type of light aerobic exercise, such as brisk walking, light jogging, bike riding, or using a rowing or elliptical machine. One very important thing to keep in mind is to avoid holding your breath while engaging in resistance training exercises. Restricting your oxygen intake while lifting heavy loads will increase your blood pressure. This can be dangerous for those who suffer from hypertension, so make sure to breathe regularly while lifting.

Strength Training Schedule						
Exercises	(3) Sets		(2)	(1) Load		(4) Freq.
	Beg.	Exp.	Rep.	Beg.	Exp.	Days/Week
Squats	1–2	2–3	8 - 12	Mod.	Hard to Very Hard	2 - 3
Push-ups	1–2	2–3	8 - 12	Mod.	Hard to Very Hard	2 - 3
Lunges	1–2	2–3	8 - 12	Mod.	Hard to Very Hard	2 - 3
Lats	1–2	2–3	8 - 12	Mod.	Hard to Very Hard	2 - 3
Row	1–2	2–3	8 - 12	Mod.	Hard to Very Hard	2 - 3
Leg Press (machine)	1–2	2–3	8 - 12	Mod.	Hard to Very Hard	2 - 3
Abdominals	1–2	2–3	10 - 15	Low-Mod.	Hard	2 - 3
Military Press (shoulders)	1–2	2–3	10 - 15	Low-Mod.	Hard	2 - 3
Lateral Raises (shoulders)	1–2	2–3	10 - 15	Low-Mod.	Hard	2 - 3
Posterior Deltoid (shoulders)	1–2	2–3	10 - 15	Low-Mod.	Hard	2 - 3
Biceps Curls	1–2	2–3	10 - 15	Low-Mod.	Hard	2 - 3
Triceps Extension	1–2	2–3	10 - 15	Low-Mod.	Hard	2 - 3

Beg.: Beginners; **Exp.:** Experienced; **Mod.:** Moderate. **Load:** use resistance that will allow you to complete 8-12 repetitions with a load to near exhaustion.

(1) Means that Loads is the first variable to increase for a proper progression.

(2) Means that Repetitions per Set is the second variable to increase for a proper progression

(3) Means that Sets is the third variable to increase for a proper progression.

(4) Means that Frequency is the fourth variable to increase for a proper progression.

Table 1

Runner-Specific Strength Training Exercises

Increased strength in certain hip muscles (abductors and external rotators) has been found to decrease injuries in runners.[44] Additionally, according to Drs. Robert Maschi and Heather Williams, authors of *"A Runner's Guide to*

Plyometrics and Core Strength Training,"[43] having good core stability is the basis of injury-free running. The authors emphasize that the core muscles comprise more than just the abdominals; they also include the hip muscles, gluteus medius, and gluteus maximus, which are the most important in stabilizing the pelvis. These muscles need to be individually strengthened to maintain good form during running.

Core Stability

The following training schedule will address this issue, increasing strength in the weaker muscles of the pelvis, which play an important role in maintaining neutral position while running.

Core Stability Exercises					
Exercises	**(2) Sets**	**(1) Rep./ Hold**	**(4)Progression**		**(3) Freq.**
			Intermediate	**Experienced**	
Side Steps	1–3	10-30			2 - 3
Step-ups	1–3	10-15	knee up	hand weights	2 - 3
Back/Gluteus	1–3	20-30"			2 - 3
Plank	1–3	20-60"			2 - 3
Bridge (1 and 2)	1–3	30-60"	knee up (1)	on forearms (2)	2 - 3
Side Plank	1–3	10-15	extend arm up	reach under	2 - 3
Reverse Curl (abs)	1–3	10-15	legs extended		2 - 3
Hip Extension	1–3	15-30			2 - 3
Fire Hydrant	1–3	15-30			2 - 3
Lateral kicks	1–3	15-30			2 - 3
Hip Rotation	1–3	30"			2 - 3

Rep/Hold: repetitions and holding: number of reps, and a time for holding in seconds (").

Progression: see pictures with explanation to increase difficulty. When you increase progression decrease (1), (2), and (3)

Freq.: (Frequency) days per week to repeat schedule.

(1) Means that Repetitions per Set is the first variable to increase for a proper progression.

(2) Means that Set is the second variable to increase for a proper progression.

(3) Means that Frequency is the third variable to increase for a proper progression.

(4) Means that increasing difficulty is the fourth variable to increase for a proper progression (lower reps and sets when increasing intensity though)

Table 2 (See explanation and pictures at the end of the chapter)

In addition to the exercises that enhance general muscular fitness and core stability, other types of strength training will improve performance in specific running events. For example, strength endurance seems to be important in middle distance (5 and 10k) and long distance running events (half and full marathon). Adding moderate interval training to continuous strength training (the type of exercises found in Table 1), has been found to improve strength endurance. On the other hand, explosive strength has been found to be more valuable in running events with high running velocity (the types of distances run in track: 800 m, 1500 m). This type of strength training improves running technique as well as running economy in short distance racing.[45]

Beginners: If you are a beginner in both running and strength training, do the running and resistance training on different days to prevent fatigue. If you are a veteran runner and want to start a strength training program, you can do so on running days. Do the strength training exercises before you go for a run. Since you are already accustomed to running, you can devote better attention to the new workout. A good rule of thumb for the strength training beginner is to learn proper technique from an experienced fitness professional. An expert can give you feedback on your body position and help you prevent undesired outcomes such as injuries.

Veterans: If you have experience with resistance training, you can add some running-specific exercises to your regular routine. When using strength training to enhance your running, the goal is not to increase the number or size of the recruited muscle fibers, but to enhance muscle power, which in turn, will increase your speed.

Plyometrics

On Table 3 you will find a list of exercises that use plyometrics, which is a method for developing explosive muscle power. The distances that most of you are training for (5k to 26.2 mi) do not require that you execute these exercises at maximal intensity to generate improvements in performance. For the purposes of training for longer distances, these plyometric exercises should be interjected between three or four traditional exercises to create a moderate interval training schedule.

Plyometric Exercises					
Exercises	**(2) Sets**	**(1) Reps.**	**(4) Progression**		**(3) Freq.**
			Inter.	**Exp.**	
Pogo	1–3	10-15	x		2 - 3
Fast Skipping	1–3	10-15	x		2 - 3
Box Jump	1–3	8-10	x		2 - 3
Stairs s	1–3	10-15	x		2 - 3
Stairs d	1–3	4-6		x	2 - 3
Lateral Step Jump	1–3	10-15	x		2 - 3
Step Touch	1–3	10-15	x		2 - 3
Lateral Jump	1–3	6-8	x		2 - 3
Diagonal Jump	1–3	8-10		x	2 - 3
Side Hop	1–3	4-6		x	2 - 3
Power Lunge	1–3	4-6		x	2 - 3

Reps.: number of repetitions per set.

Progression: intermediates should start with the exercises that have an x in that column; then try the experienced ones after 4-6 weeks. When you try a higher intensity exercise, decrease the reps, sets and frequency at the beginning.

Freq.: (Frequency) days per week to repeat schedule.

(1) Means that Repetitions per Set is the first variable to increase for a proper progression.

(2) Means that Set is the second variable to increase for a proper progression.

(3) Means that Frequency is the third variable to increase for a proper progression.

(4) Means that increasing difficulty is the fourth variable to increase for a proper progression. (Lower reps when increasing intensity though).

Table 3 (See explanation and pictures at the end of the chapter)

For example, if you follow the traditional resistance training schedule, you will perform two sets each of squats, push-ups and lunges before doing one of the exercises listed in table 3, such as "box jump." Afterward, you will resort back to the traditional schedule for another three exercises. Following that cluster of exercises, chose another plyometric exercise from the list, such as "stairs" (see Table 4).

Interval Training

This interval training schedule is best suited for those with some resistance training experience who want to improve running performance. The schedule includes only intermediate plyometric exercises (in light grey shade), but as soon as you have increased the number of repetitions and sets suggested and are proficient at executing these exercises, you can advance by substituting the intermediate exercises for the experienced ones (power lunge, side hop, etc.). Start with the lowest number of reps and sets, and progress every three to four weeks.

Interval Training		
Exercises	**(2) Sets**	**(1) Reps.**
Squats	2–3	8 - 12
Push-ups	2–3	8 - 12
Lunges	2–3	8 - 12
Box Jump	1–3	10 - 15
Lats	2–3	8 - 12
Row	2–3	8 - 12
Leg Press (machine)	2–3	8 - 12
Step Touch/Side Hop	1–3	7 - 10
Abdominals	2–3	10 - 15
Military Press (shoulders)	2–3	10 - 15
Lateral Raises (shoulders)	2–3	10 - 15
Stairs (s)/Lateral Jump	1–3	10 - 15
Posterior Deltoid (shoulders)	2–3	10 - 15
Biceps Curls	2–3	10 - 15
Triceps Extension	2–3	10 - 15
Pogo/Fast Skipping	1–3	8 - 10
Abs (upper, lower and obliques)	1-3	12-20
(1) Means that Repetitions per Set is the first variable to increase for a proper progression.		
(2) Means that Set is the second variable to increase for a proper progression.		

Table 4

Flexibility

The goal of flexibility training is to maintain normal range of motion, which reduces the chance of muscle imbalances, thus decreasing the likelihood of injury. Two of the most common stretches used to enhance flexibility are dynamic and static. Dynamic stretches, also known as mobility drills, mimic the movement of a sport or activity, such as a walking knee lift stretch. These stretches are mostly used during the warm up, to prepare the body for the upcoming activity. Static stretches are performed slowly and held for at least 30 seconds. Static stretching can be active or passive. Active static stretching involves holding the stretched position using the strength of the agonist muscle, which is common in many forms of yoga. In passive static stretching, a position is assumed while holding a limb or other part of the body with or without the assistance of a partner or device (such as elastic bands or a barre). In general, flexibility training should be performed after a good warm up or after endurance or strength training exercises. Static stretching should follow the warm up, because stretching cold muscles can cause injury. It is best performed within five to ten minutes after practicing a sport or activity, in order to take full advantage of the increased muscle temperature.[46] Given some personal variation, the most common muscles that runners need to stretch are: calves, hamstrings, hip flexors, gluteus, and quadriceps. Most importantly, flexibility exercises may enhance postural stability and balance, particularly when combined with resistance exercise. A well rounded flexibility routine shouldn't take more than ten minutes for most people.

Flexibility Exercises			
Muscle Stretched	**(2) Time**	**(1) Reps.**	**(3) Freq.**
Calves	10–30"	2 to 4	2 - 3
Hamstring	10–30"	2 to 4	2 - 3
Quadriceps	10–30"	2 to 4	2 - 3
Hip Flexor	10–30"	2 to 4	2 - 3
Lower Back	10–30"	2 to 4	2 - 3
Fascia Lata	10–30"	2 to 4	2 - 3
Piriformis	10–30"	2 to 4	2 - 3
Groin (Sartorius)	10–30"	2 to 4	2 - 3
(1) Means that Repetitions per Set is the first variable to increase for a proper progression.			
(2) Means that Time is the second variable to increase for a proper progression.			
(3) Means that Frequency is the third variable to increase for a proper progression.			

The ACSM[42] recommendations for adults seeking general flexibility with associated health benefits are as follows:

Flexibility Training

- *Frequency:* 2–3 days a week; best results will occur with daily exercise
- *Intensity:* stretch to the point of feeling tightness or slight discomfort
- *Time:* hold a static stretch for 10–30 seconds
- *Type:* a series of flexibility exercises (static flexibility- active or passive, and dynamic flexibility) for each of the major muscles
- *Volume:* a reasonable target is to perform 60 seconds of total stretching time for each flexibility exercise
- *Repetition:* repeat each exercise 2-4 times per session
- *When:* perform each flexibility exercise when the muscle temperature is elevated, preferably after cardiorespiratory or resistance exercise

Core Stabilization Exercises Explanation

Side Steps:

Equipment: elastic loop

Place an elastic band around your ankles. Standing up, with hips and knees slightly bent, gluteus and belly contracted, proceed to step to the side while maintaining the position. Always keep some tension on the band and do not extend at the hip or knees.

Perform 1-3 sets of 10-15 reps in each direction.

Step-ups:

Equipment: sturdy bench or lower step of stairs between 6 to 18 inches

Beginner: Stand up facing the bench/stairs and step up with one leg, using the top leg to lift your body weight instead of pushing off with the bottom leg. While stepping up, extend the leg completely (do not hyperextend though), contracting the gluteus (pic #2). Lower yourself slowly, controlling the movement of bending the acting leg until you step down with the back leg.

Intermediate: Bring the knee up when you step (pic 3).

Advanced: Add hand held weights.

Perform 1-3 sets of 10-15 reps on each leg.

Back/Gluteus:

Lie face down with your arms stretched forward, and your gluteus and belly contracted. Keeping your forehead on the floor, lift one arm with palm  towards the ceiling up to your ear. At the same time, lift the opposite leg. Hold your arm and opposite leg in this position for 20-30 seconds. Return arm and leg to resting position and perform with the other arm and leg. Repeat once again for each side.

Plank:

With your belly facing the floor, stand on all fours on your forearms and toes, forming a tight bridge (do not raise the hips). Contract the gluteus and abdomen. Hold 20-60 seconds.

Bridge 1:

Beginner: On your back with knees bent and heels on the floor, contract the gluteus and abdomen and lift the hips up to the ceiling until only the shoulders and heels are on the floor (pic 1). Return to resting.

Intermediate: Lift one leg while performing the bridge (pic 2).

Perform 1-3 sets of 10-30 reps (on each side for intermediate exercise).

Bridge 2:

Resting on the forearms with belly facing up and legs spread slightly, hip-width, raise and contract the gluteus. Hold 30-60 seconds.

Side Plank:

Beginner: Lie on your side with legs straight, the top leg in front and the bottom leg behind. Leaning on one elbow, lift and lower your hips.

Intermediate: Extend the top arm towards the ceiling as you lift and lower hips

Advanced: "Dive" the arm under the body across the chest, twisting your torso towards the mat and rotating your feet during each "dive."(Do not lift nor lower hips).

Perform 10 - 15 reps on each side for any level.

Reverse Curl (abs):

Lying on your back, extend the arms over the head and grab the mat.

Beginner: Lift the legs and cross them, then lift the hips up to the ceiling, bringing the legs over to your head. Lower the hips slowly back to the mat.

Intermediate: Same as above, this time keep the legs extended, and when you lower the hips, lower the legs towards the mat as well, making sure you don't arch your lower back.

Perform 10 - 30 reps for each level.

Hip Extension:

On all fours, gluteus and abdomen contracted, raise one heel towards the ceiling keeping your knee bent at a 90 degree angle so that the quad is facing the mat. In this position, move your leg up and down in small and controlled movements initiated from the muscle strength of the gluteus (avoid using momentum).

Perform 15 - 30 reps on each leg.

Fire Hydrant (variation of Hip Extension):

Begin on all fours on the mat, then lift your knee out to the side keeping a 90 degree bend in your knee until your inner thigh is parallel with the mat.

Perform 15 - 30 reps on each leg.

Lateral Kicks (variation of Fire Hydrant):

On all fours, lift your knee out sideways. Maintaining this position, push the heel back to extend the leg behind you, keeping the sides of the knee and foot parallel to the floor. Return to bent knee.

Perform 10 - 15 reps on each leg.

Hip Rotation (TV position):

Get comfortable laying on your side with legs bent and head resting on your bottom arm. Pivot the top knee inward and lift the sole of your foot towards the ceiling.

Move #1: (knee to knee)

Pulse the sole of your foot up towards the ceiling and back down for 30 seconds, keeping your knee bent so that your leg is almost making a 90 degree angle throughout the move. Repeat on other leg.

Perform pulses for 30 sec on each leg.

Move #2: (knee, kick to wall)

Keep the top knee pivoted inwards and sole of foot facing the ceiling to start so that your leg forms a 90 degree angle. Extend your leg so that you kick the sole of your foot towards the wall and so your top leg becomes parallel to the ground. Then bring the sole of your foot back up to face the ceiling.

Perform exercise for 30 sec on each leg.

Move #3: (knee, kick to ceiling)

This move is similar to # 2, but this time, use larger movements to push the heel up towards the ceiling and out towards the wall so that your top leg creates a straight diagonal line from your hip out to the wall. Rotate the thigh back inward to bring the sole of the foot back to resting position facing the ceiling.

Perform exercise for 30 sec on each leg.

Plyometrics Exercises Explanation

Pogo:

This is a jump-in-place exercise to practice lower leg and ankle extension and quick contact and elastic takeoff. Standing with hips and knees slightly bent, propel yourself upwards using your arms to create momentum. Keep your feet flexed (not pointed towards the floor), and slap the ground when landing. Take off again right away, using the elasticity of the leg muscles to jump up again.

Perform 1-3 sets of 20-30 jumps.

Galloping:

This drill is great practice for the takeoff part of running. It emphasizes extending the back leg and ankle to give you that extra ump in your stride. Start by standing with one leg slightly forward and push off with the back leg and foot. Keeping the same leg back, project your hips and the opposite leg forward. Use your arms for balance and to help you propel forward. Repeat 10-15 times on one side; then change legs.

Perform 1-3 sets on each side.

Fast Skipping:

The purpose of this drill is to enhance stride frequency, extension of the pushing leg, and power in the takeoff. Start with a double hop on one leg, driving the other knee up and forward. Keep the strides short and push off with force, but do not go for height. Instead, stay close to the floor, as if jumping in place one leg at a time. Fully extend the push-off leg before hoping again.

Perform 1-3 sets of 20-30 jumps.

Stairs s (single leg):

Similar to the Box Jump, this drill enhances takeoff and soft landing by improving balance on the landing leg. Find stairs with 10 or more closed steps and run up them. Accentuate the takeoff by fully extending the bottom leg and landing softly on the front leg. To increase intensity, run up 2 steps at a time.

Run up 10-20 stairs 1-3 times.

Stairs d (double legs):

Same as single stairs, but this time with both feet together. This is also a variation of the Box Jump (see in next pages), used to develop a powerful takeoff. Start by assuming a semi-squat position, keeping your arms relaxed at your sides. Jump up, fully extending the legs and land softly with bent knees, ready for the next jump.

Repeat 5-10 times for 1-3 sets.

Step Touch:

Equipment: sturdy bench or lower step of stairs about 6 inches high.

This drill is also for enhancing stride frequency and power in the takeoff. Start by standing in a relaxed position facing the step. Then, keeping the belly tight, begin tapping the step with alternating feet. Increase your speed until you are airborne with each tap.

Perform 1-3 sets of 20-30" jumps.(Maintain a controlled speed)

Box Jump:

Equipment: sturdy bench or lower step of stairs between 6 to 18 inches.

If you are jumping on a box or step, make sure that the equipment won't slide when you jump on it. The purpose of this drill is to recruit many muscle fibers and to learn how to land softly on a hard surface, using those muscles to brace the impact the way you would while running. Stand close to the step, bend the legs slightly, and bring the arms down and backwards, to draw momentum as you begin to jump up and forward onto the box. Make sure you land with both feet completely on top of the step; don't let your heels hang off. It's also important to make sure you land softly, bracing yourself with your muscles. Step down and repeat 10 times. To increase intensity, you can jump down and quickly up again.

Perform 1-3 sets of 10 reps.

Lateral Jump:

This drill also emphasizes takeoff and full leg extension, adding lateral muscles to those most commonly used in running. In this exercise, focus on using your hips and lower back in addition to the thigh and groin muscles. Starting in a semi-squat position, push off with the outside leg, shifting your weight in the opposite direction and projecting your body laterally. Use force in the push-off and land softly on the inside leg with the knee bent. Make sure the knee stays forward and do not move laterally. Immediately take off again towards the side you just came from.

Perform 1-3 sets of 10-15 reps.

Diagonal Jump:

Same as Lateral Jump, except jump forward in a diagonal (either across or to the side). As with the Lateral Jump, put care into keeping the landing knee bent and forward-facing; do not let it move inward or laterally. Land softly.

Perform 1-3 sets of 10-15 reps.

Lateral Step Jump:

Equipment: sturdy bench or lower step of stairs between 6 to 10 inches.

As with the Box Jump, start in a semi-squat position with the arms relaxed at your sides. This time, jump up and to the side, landing softly with bent knees and both feet fully on the step. Gently step down, or jump down and quickly up again for increased intensity.

Perform 1-3 sets of 10-15 reps.

Side Hop:

Similar to the Lateral Step Jump and Lateral Jump, this drill emphasizes takeoff, soft landing, and the use of the hips and lower back muscles. You can use a mark on the floor or a plastic cone to jump over laterally. Start in a semi-squat position with arms relaxed at your sides

and jump laterally with both feet together. Use force to propel yourself over the mark or cone, landing softly and with knees bent. Use your arms to help gain height. Immediately jump back to where you started for increased intensity, or recover for a few seconds before jumping again.

Perform 1-3 sets of 10-15 reps.

Power Lunge:

This drill enhances speed and power in the lower body. Start in a lunge position with one leg extended forward and bent so that the knee is directly above the ankle. Bend the back leg with the knee

underneath the hips and pointing towards the floor. Using your arms to help you gain height, jump as high as you can, reversing the position of your legs at the top of the jump. Land softly in the starting position and take off again immediately. Focus on attaining height and speed in the movement.

Perform 1-3 sets of 10-15 reps.

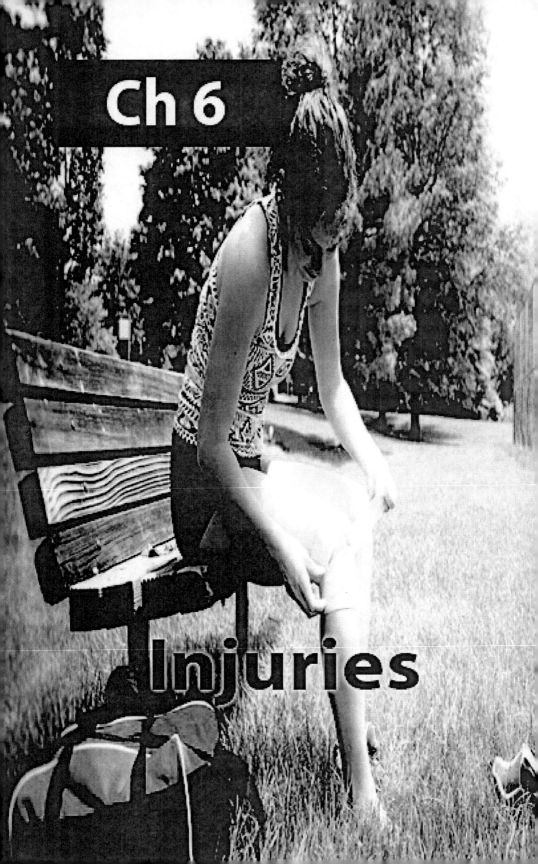

Ch 6

Injuries

Muscle soreness is going to happen while running, and it has been found to be a good tool for monitoring exercise intensity for the recreational female runner.[47] "I'm not a fan of the 'no pain-no gain' mantra," says Ellen Seuffert, R.N., F.N.P, from Westfield Family Practice in NJ. "Pain and ache are different, though," she adds. The kind of pain that is accompanied by swelling, redness, stiffness or fever is not good. On the other hand, aches can be "stretched out, showered out, and 'advil-ed' out," according to Seuffert. She advises to listen to your body, which will let you know when to stop.

While exercising, there are two types of muscle soreness: the kind you feel right after exercise (acute soreness), and delayed onset muscle soreness (DOMS). The first type, felt during or right after exercise, is due to a buildup of lactic acid, a by-product of muscular exhaustion, and it disappears a few hours after training. On the other hand, DOMS develops a day or two after a high intensity training session. Additionally, DOMS will negatively affect running performance.[7, 48] Therefore, if you experience DOMS and a decrease in running performance, you might be hearing the bells that signal the beginning of overtraining.

Overtraining is doing too much, too soon. Symptoms of overtraining besides a decrease in performance are: sleep disturbances (either sleeping too much or insomnia), lack of appetite, chronic fatigue, and an increase in the heart rate's response to a given intensity and duration. Moreover, overtraining is the number one cause of musculoskeletal and bone stress injuries in runners, and unfortunately, if you are a novice runner, your chances of getting injured are a bit higher than if you are a veteran. In most cases, this is due to an inappropriate training program. There are other factors that may contribute to the risk of injury, including poor technique, ill-fitting footwear, menstrual irregularities, and low bone mineral density, but these causes are less dangerous than an inappropriate training program.[49, 50, 51]

You should consider consulting your physician if:

- Muscle or joint pain is sharp and persistent
- You are feeling continually tired

You should **immediately** consult a physician if:

- You feel pain or discomfort in the chest, neck, jaw, upper back, or upper abdominal area while exercising that disappears with rest. These could be symptoms of cardiac disease.

To avoid injury and muscle soreness, start your training and exercise session very slowly and progressively build up. Adding a cool-down at the end of a training session will help diffuse the molecular by-products created in the muscle during exercise, reducing discomfort and soreness.

Scaling back on training or stopping training altogether are the typical remedies for overtraining. If you suspect you have been overtraining, it is important that you seek medical advice right away. Inform your physician of your personal history and recent exercise performance, and request for a thorough clinical examination.[52]

Injuries

Among runners, the most frequently injured body parts vary by running level and experience (e.g., novice, recreational, marathoner). In general, injuries are most regularly reported in the lower leg, knee and ankle/foot. Common risk factors across different running levels include age, running history and injury history. Typical injuries among novice runners include the lower leg, knee and ankle/foot. For the recreational runner, most injuries occur in the ankle/foot, knee, and lower leg. Finally, the most frequently injured areas for marathoners are the knee, ankle/foot, and thigh.[53]

Here are some common injuries and ways to prevent them:

Achilles Tendonitis (inflammation of the Achilles tendon): This is the most common injury sustained by long-distance runners and middle-aged runners. Overuse and poor calf muscle flexibility seem to be the major causes of this condition. The athlete should modify his/her training by decreasing mileage and avoiding a fast pace, hills and uneven surfaces running until the pain subsides. Proper fitting shoes should help reduce the incidence of tendonitis.[54]

Shin Splints: This type of injury is characterized by tenderness in the front of the lower leg. The pain typically occurs upon commencing activity and disappears as the athlete warms up into their running, only to reappear during cool-down. The incidence of shin splints is significantly higher in novice and recreational runners than in marathoners, competitive runners, and cross-country athletes. Additionally, women seem to be affected by this type of injury more often than men.

Excessive pronation (inward rotation of the foot) and rear foot valgus (a condition in which the rear of the foot tends to curve outwards at the ankle joint) are the most common causes of shin splints. Improper footwear, sudden increases in frequency and/or intensity within an exercise regimen, uneven surfaces, and low calcium intake may also lead to shin splints.[55] If training continues and the injury progresses, pain becomes more constant throughout a running session and the athlete may need to stop because of the severity of the pain.

Management of fractures and stress reactions in the bone (shin) involves reducing impact loading (running/jumping) until the pain resolves. During this period, the athlete may cross-train through nonimpact activities, such as cycling, swimming and elliptical machines. After developing shin splints, a runner should only slowly resume running when they are pain-free.[49] The use of orthotic inserts has also been found to help with this ailment.[51, 53]

Plantar Fasciitis (inflammation of the plantar fascia): The telltale sign of this injury is morning pain in the thick band of tissue on the bottom of the foot. The pain is typically worst with the first step out of bed and gradually gets better throughout the day.[54] This inflammation is common among long distance runners and those who have arch problems (flat feet or overly high arches), also wearing shoes with poor arch support has been found to contribute to this condition.

As with any injury, talk to your doctor before starting a recovery plan; in the meantime, rest and apply ice to the inflamed area. Sometimes a better shoe will make a difference, and orthotic inserts can also help. Athletes with plantar fasciitis should reduce total mileage and incorporate softer arch support, as well as avoid uneven surfaces. Incorporating a prolonged warm-up, especially of the foot, and stretching the arch before running can help to reduce tenderness. Additionally, ice should be applied immediately after runs. If there is no relief with these interventions, running should be stopped altogether, and the athlete should find an alternative aerobic non-impact activity to prevent loss of fitness until the pain is gone.

Knee Pain: The causes of knee pain vary, but about 50% of the time it can be attributed to misalignment. Misalignment results from imbalances in the forces that control the position of the knee cap (patella) during knee flexion and extension, especially when the joint is carrying weight. Excessive pronation (inward rotation of the foot), imbalanced leg muscle strength, (usually the quadriceps are stronger than the hamstrings), and lateral quadriceps tightness are the major causes.

Patellofemoral syndrome is characterized by anterior knee pain accompanied by a "grinding" sensation. The tale-tell sign of this condition is pain after

being seated for a long time. Another common source of knee pain is patellar tendonitis. This condition is characterized by pain in the upper portion of the knee cap, where the quadriceps tendon inserts into the patella. Running uphill or jumping intensifies the symptoms.

Lateral knee pain is typically attributed to iliotibial band syndrome. The iliotibial band is a thickening of the fascia, or the outer casing of the muscle, that runs up the outside of the thigh. It originates up by the top of the hip and ends on the outside of the knee. When the band becomes tight, it snaps during continuous flexion and extension of the knee. This condition is aggravated when running downhill, on slanted roads, or with sudden increases in the intensity or volume of training.[54] Treatment for knee pain will most likely include reducing inflammation of the injured tissues and rehabilitation of the weak muscles to restore joint balance and stability.

Hip Pain: In addition to knee pain, iliotibial band syndrome can also cause discomfort in the hips. In this case, tightness in the iliotibial band produces sharp or burning pain in the hip that is exacerbated by activity.[56] Iliotibial band syndrome is typically due to overuse. Muscle weakness (gluteus medius) around the joints can also contribute to this type of pain. As described in the strength training chapter, including hip abduction exercises into your routine may help prevent this issue. If hip pain remains a problem, talk to your doctor. He or she will most likely prescribe physical therapy to alleviate the symptoms and demonstrate the necessary corrective exercises.

Other Conditions

The Female Athlete Triad: Most commonly known as Triad, is a condition consisting of insufficient energy availability (often tied to an eating disorder), amenorrhea (absence of menstrual period), and osteoporosis.[7] Prolonged insufficient energy availability can carry many health problems, not only physical but mental as well, including cardiovascular and skeletal issues, anxiety and depression. Amenorrheic athletes are infertile and, due to a decreased secretion of the hormone estrogen, they can develop many health irregularities. These include reduced blood delivery to the working muscles and defective muscular metabolism, both of which are essential to an athlete's performance. Lastly, osteoporosis is closely related to amenorrhea. The more menstrual cycles missed, the less dense the bones become, and the danger in this is that loss of bone mineral density can become irreversible. Prevention of the Triad is the best approach. Taking calcium and vitamin D as well as including strength training regularly in your exercise regime should help you to maintain healthy bone density. Additionally, athletes with amenorrhea and/or eating disorders should seek medical counseling (general physician, dietician and/or mental health specialist) immediately to prevent further damages to the system.

Incontinence: Female Urinary Incontinence (FUI) is a condition in which a woman has difficulty controlling or cannot control her bladder, either during exercise or at all times. It is prevalent in 14-31% of women and can have very negative effects on quality of life. A common theme in this condition is the lack of cases in which professional intervention is sought.[57] Some of the risk factors for FUI include age, body mass index, the number of babies delivered, and diabetes.[58] Unfortunately, FUI may limit exercise participation. Luckily for some women, simple measures, like long-term,  moderate physical activity[59] and pelvic floor exercises,[60] can help improve the condition. Nevertheless, early and correct diagnosis of incontinence is essential to finding the right treatment.[61]

If you still tinkle while you run, you can wear a pad and one of those trendy running skorts. Not only will you look great, but you will be able to run free and happy again!

Gastrointestinal (GI) Discomfort: GI symptoms vary from person to person, and the intake of different types of carbohydrates, in the form of gels and or fluids, will have a different effect on each runner. Lower GI symptoms such as diarrhea, gas, and abdominal pain are common during running, especially if the runner consumes carbs during exercise.[62] There are many mechanisms that can cause GI discomfort, like gastroesophageal reflux, GI dysmotility, and decreased GI blood flow.[63] Consuming carbs while exercising is one of the causes for GI discomfort.[64] Drinking water before exercise and eating solid foods during exercise, especially fatty, high-fiber foods, can also provoke GI discomfort. Individual testing of food and drink intake during exercise are vital to alleviating lower GI symptoms.[62]

Hyponatremia: Also known as water intoxication, hyponatremia occurs when an excess consumption of water results in a reduction of electrolytes at the cellular level. The symptoms are similar to those of heat exhaustion: nausea, muscle cramps and confusion. Even though it is a rare condition, it is important to take it into consideration.[64] During prolonged exercise or in hot and humid conditions, sports drinks are better than water for rehydration because continuous rehydration can only be achieved by replacing the electrolytes lost in sweat.[66]

Heat-related Illness: Factors that can put one at risk for heat illness can be internal, like medications or poor fitness, or external, like temperature, humidity, and the intensity and duration of exercise. Heat illness can range from a mild prickly heat, in which a skin eruption arises from clogged sweat glands, to heat stroke, which is a serious condition that requires medical attention. Heat cramps (cramping of the big muscles) are usually a result of mild dehydration, which can develop into the more serious condition of heat exhaustion if not treated. Heat exhaustion occurs when athletes become dehydrated and cannot dissipate their heat effectively. Profuse sweating, headache, nausea, and intense fatigue are signs of heat exhaustion, and if they are not addressed, the condition can quickly progress to heat stroke. Heat stroke is a medical emergency that can be deadly if untreated. Prompt external cooling is critical to reducing further damage from heat. Preventing heat illness is often as easy as staying well-hydrated, wearing cooling clothing, like hats and shirts made out of wicking materials, and being physically fit.[67]

Runny Nose/Virus Infection: According to Seuffert, "Running with a runny nose is one thing, but running with chest congestion, shortness of breath, fever, sore throat, or any GI symptoms is not a good idea." She compares running with a viral infection to driving a car without gas: you won't get very far and it's not very good for the engine.

Diabetes: If you suffer from diabetes, Seuffert recommends talking to your primary health care provider before beginning any exercise program. That said, she emphasizes that diabetics, Types I and II, can benefit from regular exercise. She suggests starting with a walking regime and slowly increasing speed and distance, taking great care not to progress prematurely. "Nothing ruins an exercise regime faster than an injury, be it from low blood sugar or incurring a musculoskeletal injury," she adds. A great read for those who want more information on diabetes and athletics is Dr. Sheri Colberg's book *"Diabetic Athlete's Handbook."*

Skin Lesions: Running can cause many types of sores due to the friction of clothing against the skin. Some examples include:

Chafing: Chafing commonly appears around an ill-fitting bra or the seams of underwear, especially when wet. Applying petroleum-based jelly or Body Glide in the areas susceptible to chafing can prevent this inconvenience. Nowadays, there are many options in underwear, including seamless underwear made out of wicking material, which is a great alternative to cotton.

Blisters: Blisters are the result of repetitive friction that frequently occur if the shoes are too big or too tight, or the area is moist.[68] Wearing well-fitting shoes and socks made from wicking material is the best barrier against blister development.[69] Although moist skin increases chafing, very dry or very wet skin decreases chafing. Try to keep your feet dry on dry days, but do not worry too much in the rain: the excess moisture will decrease the friction forces and impede blister formation. Additionally, if you are a beginner, your skin will eventually adapt to the repeated friction by thickening the areas of contact and reducing the likelihood of blisters.[70]

Jogger's Toes: Black toenails are the result of the toes' repeated contact with the shoe box. This doesn't necessarily mean that the shoe is the culprit; sometimes, this condition develops with well-fitting shoes. In some cases, the problem is the lacing. Shoes should be tightly laced to prevent the foot from sliding forward, but not so tightly that circulation is cut off. The shoe box should accommodate the toes comfortably. Finally, keeping the toenails trimmed in a straight line (not curved) will help prevent jogger's toes.[71]

Skin Cancer: It is estimated that 65-90% cases of melanoma are caused by UV exposure.[72] Practicing sports outdoors increases the risk of skin melanoma in athletes not only because of increased sun exposure, but also because sweat increases the skin's photosensitivity and heightens the risk of burns. Ellen Seuffert recommends wearing a minimum of SPF 15 sunscreen, applied 30 minutes prior to sun exposure. Wearing water-resistant sunscreen and UV-resistant clothing should reduce the risk of sunburn and skin cancer.[73]

Ch 7

What If?

Y ou have the best intentions for training and racing, but now it's raining, you are injured, it's too cold, it's too hot, etc. These types of conundrums will likely occur, especially if you are training for a long distance race. It is inevitable that while training and racing there will always be *what ifs…*

Q: What if I have to cross-train? What are the best alternatives to running?

A: Two exercises that are closely related to running and provide similar training intensities with little impact on your joints are deep water running (DWR) and the use of an elliptical machine.

As its name implies, DWR is running in water deep enough that the feet do not touch the bottom. The runner attaches a flotation belt around his/her waist, and jogs suspended in the water. DWR not only serves as a cross-training activity for those seeking an alternative cardiovascular exercise; it's also ideal for the injured athlete. Research has demonstrated that runners who substituted one normal (ground) running session for a DWR one over seven weeks period of time showed improved performance in a 5k time trial.[74] However, with DWR, the joints, especially the hip, are moved to a greater extent than with ground running. As such, athletes with certain injuries (i.e., hip or knee issues)

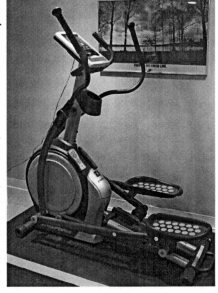

should use caution not to exacerbate the injury if using DWR as a mode of rehabilitation or fitness maintenance. DWR takes some time and skill to learn, but according to Kindling *et* al., who compared the body movements of endurance runners in deep water and on the ground, "with appropriate familiarization with exercising in a water environment, individuals should be able to benefit from DWR without risk of further injury."[75]

Using an elliptical machine is also

a viable alternative to running on the ground and may serve as a mode of rehabilitation after injury. Attaining the same intensity as running can be difficult on an elliptical machine, and your VO_2 max (maximal oxygen uptake) may decline while using the elliptical for rehabilitation. However, your VO_2 max will not drop as low as it would if you were to stop exercising altogether, which is why elliptical exercise is a great tool for short-term cross-training and recovery.[76]

Q: What if I feel I'm too old to run, especially a marathon?

A: Allow me to share a statistic from the results of the November 2011 New York City Marathon. The oldest person to finish this race was an 84-year-old woman, who managed to complete the 26.2 miles in 7:44 hours. Considering this, if you are younger than 84, I would try to find another excuse not to run! In all seriousness, it's clear from this woman's time that she did quite a bit of walking during the marathon, and that's what's important to keep in mind. You don't have to run for the entire race in order to finish on time. As we discussed in Chapter 4, the right amount of training, along with alternating between jogging and walking, will allow you to maintain a comfortable intensity level no matter what your age. Leyk *et* al., the authors of the study, "Physical performance in middle age and old age: good news for our sedentary and aging society," suggest that, "performance losses in middle age are mainly due to a sedentary lifestyle rather than biological aging."[77] Moreover, they claim that advanced age is not an impediment to achieving high levels of performance if an athlete trains regularly. If that's not enough incentive, running at an advanced age has been found to be a safe and rewarding choice to enhance health in the aging population.[78] So, lace up those running shoes, and off you go!

Q: What if there's snow or ice on the road?

A: One option is to run inside, using a treadmill, but if it's a long run, this may be tedious or monotonous. Thus, you may want to consider venturing outside with traction devices over your regular running shoes. If you do use a treadmill, keep in mind that it's easier than running on the ground, but you can use that specific training session to work on speed, pace or tempo, for example.

Use 1 to 2 % elevation to mimic ground elevation, and make sure there is enough ventilation in the room to prevent overheating.

Trail running can be a great addition to your training program, but be aware that it's more difficult than road running. Wear trail running shoes, which have more traction than regular running shoes and are sturdier to protect your feet against rocks and roots.

If you have to run on snowy or icy streets, you can use traction devices. These are accessories that you attach over your running shoes to keep from slipping and sliding (see more about this in the Gadgets Chapter).

Be advised that running on ice or snow will take more effort than regular road running, so don't be upset if you don't cover the usual distance in the usual time. You'll still be able to achieve a good exercise session, if not a better one, due to the recruiting of stabilizer muscles you don't usually need when running on a leveled, stable surface. Be super careful though: start slow and easy, and go back home if you don't feel safe.

Q: What if it's raining or hot and humid?

A: Cold rain showers, rain storms and thunder keep me indoors, but I'll brave most other types of weather in order to run outside. When it's wet, I wear tight-fitting clothes to prevent chaffing, including seamless "boy short" underwear made out of wicking material and tight-fitting synthetic socks to minimize the chance of blisters.

If you choose to run on hot and humid days, just be a little extra cautious, especially on your long run days. Humidity affects the body's ability to dissipate heat, so it's easy to overheat on humid days. It's also important to stay hydrated before, during, and after your run, as muggy weather will cause you to sweat more. Depending on your heart rate's response to the environment, you might have to cut your run short, on especially hot and humid days.

If your race happens to fall on a hot and humid day, you may need to revise your goals, especially if you have a time goal. Unless you have trained in worse elements, heat and humidity will affect your outcome, mostly negatively. So take it easy, listen to your body (not the clock), and be flexible with your personal goals. Trying to keep a pace that you established in moderate temperatures will be incredibly hard (and potentially dangerous) on a hot and humid day. Trust me, and give yourself some slack in extreme weather; you will be glad you did.

Q: What if it's too cold?

A: Exercise increases your metabolism, and thus your body temperature. This, combined with some extra clothing, will ensure that you stay nice and cozy on a cold winter day. However, make sure you layer clothing that allows for evaporation, to keep you both warm and dry. Be careful not to pile on too much clothing or you might suffer from what is called a "tropical person" in a cold environment, wherein you end up overheating despite the chilly temperatures. Layer on clothing so you can gradually remove pieces as your body temperature increases.[79] One piece of clothing I started using in the last few years are arm warmers. These are just sleeves, they just cover your arms, and when you are warm enough to wear only a T-shirt or one long sleeve layer, you remove them and they take very little space, instead of having to carry an extra long sleeve shirt.

In very cold weather, don't forget your hat: you can lose up to 50% of your body heat through your head in temperatures 25 F or below![80] It's also

a good idea to have an extra jacket or sweatshirt ready for when you finish your workout, to prevent hypothermia as your metabolism settles back to its baseline level. Finally, make sure you keep well-hydrated. Fluid loss occurs in cold as well as hot conditions, and as we know well, dehydration will negatively impact performance.

Q: What if I get injured and I can't race?

A: This is very unfortunate, but it can happen, especially if you are training for a marathon. Most long distance races have a defer policy and a deadline for doing so. This varies from race to race, so make sure to read the fine print on the issue. If your race has a defer policy, the race director will defer your entrance until the following year, although you may have to pay a processing fee or repay the registration fee. Some races, such as the Marine Corps Marathon and the Charlotte's Thunder Road Marathon, have a transfer program. These programs permit the registered runner to switch his/her entry to a non-registered participant. Sadly, however, most races do not have a refund policy.

Q: What if I have to stop running? What should I expect when I resume?

A: Sometimes we stop running because we lose our motivation, we take on new family and/or work obligations, or we experience an injury or other health-related issues.

When there is a decline in physical activity, there is a decrease in muscle mass and the proteins that make those muscles contract, therefore, detraining ensues. The good news is that this incidence is reversible.

When we decrease our physical activity, all those muscle and skeletal adaptations that we gained during training disappear quite fast (within days!).[79] Therefore, if we try to restart our routine right where we left off, it will be quite difficult. As you probably know, it takes time and effort to achieve a certain level of fitness, so if for any reason we have to stop, picking up the pieces and getting restarted will take some time too.

Such was the case with my friend Laura Daugherty (in the picture she's running with her husband Joe and the younger two of their three kids). Laura was running 10:40 minutes per mile in half marathons, and she was quite happy and proud of that. Last summer (2011) however, Laura had a relapse in a health issue she has been dealing with for more than 10 years which required

an invasive medical procedure. Even though Laura was walking the corridors of the hospital where she was treated as soon as she got the OK from her doctors (under the frowns of some of her nurses), it is taking her a bit longer than she hoped to get back to her pre-intervention running pace. Six months after her hospitalization, Laura is struggling to keep up an 11 minute/mile pace for three miles. "It was easy to go from 15 to 12 min/mi at the beginning, but now... it is so hard to lower my 11 min./mi pace," she told me.

Yes, it is hard to bounce back, but she is doing the right thing: she is strength training twice a week and still trying to run three times a week while gaining back her strength. She is also listening to her body, and she is not asking for more than her body can give while healing. As soon as she starts feeling that she can add one or more days to her running schedule, she will see the positive difference.

In any case, if you ever have to stop running and then pick up the pieces, start slowly and be consistent. We need at least three days a week of aerobic exercise for the body to get used to the stress, as well as at least two days a week of strength training to start seeing the benefits of physical activity. If you are in very bad shape, start with simply strength training to build up some muscle mass; then slowly, three to four weeks later, add aerobic exercises. If running is too much, walk/jog until you feel that you can run the whole time. Be patient, and have faith in yourself. Think back to when you started running for the first time and where it took you. Muscles have memory, and they will remember what is like to run and will get you there as soon as they are able. You just have to give them the opportunity and the necessary tools!

Ch 8

Gadgets

Just like in any other hobby or passion, there are endless types of gadgets (and thus limitless amounts of money to spend) in the sport of running. It is up to you which are the most "critical" for you and how much to spend, but here are some gadgets to think about when buying your running accessories:

Running Strollers

According to my friends and fellow runners, Flavio and Elina Pardo, who recently had a baby girl, this is what to look for in a running stroller:

- fixed front wheel
- large 20″ high pressure tires for almost frictionless rolling and comfort
- rear suspension
- lightweight and simple but strong frame (especially important if you are running hills)

In general, all running strollers have a secure, 5-point harness, front brakes, and locking rear wheels. According to Flavio, the front brakes are basically useless, as there is almost no weight on the front wheel, so the wheel just slides; however, locking rear wheels are a MUST. Running strollers are usually harder to fold, and you'll probably have to remove all three wheels to fit it in a car trunk. The front wheel usually has a lever mechanism like a bicycle, while the rear wheels have a push button. "I would avoid models with small and swiveling front wheel," advises Flavio; "the stroller is much harder to keep straight when free, and the lockable ones hardly lock at a perfectly straight angle."

At about $450, a running stroller is no bargain. If you're seeking a lower-priced stroller, the first things you'll sacrifice are the lightweight frame (i.e., 32 lbs up from 20), and high pressure tires (although the tires can be replaced).

Snow and Ice Traction Devices

These are devices that strap to the bottom of your running shoes to give you more stability on icy or snowy surfaces. They might have steel coils, beads, spikes, or cleats, to provide extra grip. Look for a lightweight yet sturdy device that is easy to slip on but secure enough that it won't detach while you're running. Most runners prefer devices with spikes, but these are uncomfortable if you have to cross over or switch to paved surfaces. Of course, you can always remove the devices in such circumstances.

Water Bottles

On long and hot running days, don't forget your water bottle! Nowadays, there are many options for rehydrating while on the run. On especially hot days, keeping your fluids cold can be tricky. If you use a regular water bottle, one option is to fill it halfway with water or sports drink and place it in the freezer the night before your run. Before you go out for a run, top off the bottle with cold fluid, and off you go.

Some water bottles are made out of insulating material, which helps keep fluids colder a bit longer. Some also come with straps and pockets, which can hold a small phone, a gel, or your car keys. One option for carrying fluids with you is a fuel belt. These come with two to eight small bottle-holders distributed across the belt. Some also have a pocket or two. Fuel belts not only free up your hands, but they help spread out the weight of the fluid. The cons are that on hot days, the smaller amount of fluid in each bottle will heat up more quickly, and as of now, I haven't seen any of these small bottles made out insulating material. The fuel belt that I prefer (the right one in the picture)

comes with 4 water bottles, is made out of elastic material, and fastens with Velcro. I like this last detail, because I find the ones with a plastic clip irritating to my skin, and they can easily break down.

HR Monitors

These are wireless electronic devices that provide biofeedback on the level of intensity of the workout. Your heart rate is affected not only by the intensity of the workout, but also by altitude, heat and humidity, fitness level, and terrain. A heart rate monitor will help you keep an eye on your intensity level, so you can make it more efficient. (See Chapter 4 for info on heart rate threshold).

You can buy a basic heart rate monitor in any sports store or online for about $50. Polar is one of the pioneer companies for heart rate monitors, although nowadays you can find many others, such as Timex and Garmin, which also manufacture the devices. You can also find heart rate monitors on certain GPS devices or Smartphones. With the latter, you'll need to buy a Heart Rate strap and communication unit (a small device that you plug into the Smartphone).

Pedometers, GPS units and more!

There are many gadgets that will help you track your training progress. Pedometers, GPS units, and accompanying software are sometimes seen as devices reserved for the ultra-serious runners, but in truth, they are great aids for beginners as well, helping you stick to your training schedule and goals and providing the numbers to validate your achievements. But let's review them by cost and functionality.

Pedometers are the simplest devices of the bunch. They function by measuring how many steps you take during your exercise. Specifically, they detect your body's motion and convert it into steps, allowing you to determine the distance you've covered. Neat, huh? They are relatively small (fit easily in your hand or pocket), and relatively inexpensive, ranging from $5 to $50.

The simpler units will show you a display with a measure of the time elapsed and approximate distance covered during your run. Most of the higher end units are fully programmable: you can enter your stride length and weight to provide yourself with an even more accurate record of the distance covered and calories burned during your training session. Also, these upscale pedometers can be connected to a computer (most come with software and a USB cord), allowing you to upload your workouts to an electronic training log.

More sophisticated running gadgets include special Global Positioning Systems (GPS) units. In small, wristband devices, they pack the same technology used to guide cars, drawing from the signals of multiple Earth-orbiting satellites. They can determine your location very precisely (within a few feet!), and from that, measure your speed and distance covered.

The basic units start at around $80, but for about twice that price, you get a complete system that includes a heart rate monitor! Then, when you see those bpms going up, you'll be able to scientifically determine that you were really pushing it up that hill!! And of course, with all these GPS devices, you can upload and log data into your computer. I use a Garmin Forerunner 305, which monitors my heart rate, speed, distance, pace, and calories and provides a detailed post-workout analysis that I can view on my PC.

These days, many of you probably already have a Smartphone. If you do, you're probably aware that they come with a GPS embedded into their tiny body, and as they say, there is an app for that! Many entrepreneurial people have created apps that can be downloaded onto your Smartphone and convert it into a complete training companion. For example, I use Runtastic, and I find it just as useful as my wristband GPS. While the Smartphones are a bit bigger than some of the stand-alone GPS units, you'll likely be taking your phone along with you on runs anyway. You can also add a heart rate monitor to your Smartphone; for example, check out Wahoo Fitness. They provide you with a tiny communications unit that hooks up to your phone and allows it to receive information from a heart rate monitor band.

As you can see, there's a complete menu of running gadgets to choose from. You can go with the minimalist pedometer in your pocket or the full suite of electronics that will make you the envy of any mad scientist! Regardless of the variation in precision and details, these portable devices are great tools for keeping our training on track!!

Training Log

Sample Running Log						
Week	Distance	Time	Intensity	Schedule	Comments	Hours
	Mon				off		0.00
	Tues	4.5	46	easy	45		0.77
	Weds				off		0.00
	Thurs	4.7	48	easy	45		0.80
1	Fri	4.5	45	med.	45		0.75
	Sa		60	easy	off or XT	bike ride	1.00
	Su	9	93	med-hard	9 m	hot, harder than expected	1.55
	Sum	18.2	292				4.87
	Mon	3.2	35	med	35	tired from Sun run	0.58
	Tues				off		0.00
	Weds	4	41	med	40	better run than on Mon	0.68
2	Thurs				off		0.00
	Fri	4.5	45	easy	45	new shoes	0.75
	Sa	3	29		30		0.48
	Su	10	103		10 m	not as hot as last Sun, good	1.72
	Sum	21.5	253				4.22
	Mon				off		0.00
	Tues	4.5	46	med	45	good run	0.77
	Weds				off		0.00
	Thurs	5	52	easy	50	early run, need to eat better	0.87
3	Fri	4.2	40	med	40		0.67
	Sa	3.5	34	med	35	Ran with Fido	0.57
	Su	10.6	110	med-hard	11 m	good long run,	1.83
	Sum	27.8	282				4.70

Race Day Checklist

Race Day Checklist	
Running Shoes	☐
Timing Chip	☐
Running Bib	☐
Race Belt	☐
Watch, GPS, Smartphone	☐
Shorts/Pants	☐
Top	☐
Arm Warmers	☐
Socks	☐
Hat	☐
Gloves	☐
Extra Clothing for Before and After Race	☐
Hydration System	☐
Race Fuel (gels, bars)	☐
Before and After Race Snacks	☐
Sunglasses	☐
Sunscreen	☐

Pace Chart

Pace (hour:min:sec per mile)									
		08:00	08:15	08:30	08:45	09:00	09:15	09:30	09:45	10:00
Distance (miles)	3	0:24:00	0:24:45	0:25:30	0:26:15	0:27:00	0:27:45	0:28:30	0:29:15	0:30:00
	6	0:48:00	0:49:30	0:51:00	0:52:30	0:54:00	0:55:30	0:57:00	0:58:30	1:00:00
	9	1:12:00	1:14:15	1:16:30	1:18:45	1:21:00	1:23:15	1:25:30	1:27:45	1:30:00
	12	1:36:00	1:39:00	1:42:00	1:45:00	1:48:00	1:51:00	1:54:00	1:57:00	2:00:00
	13.1	1:44:48	1:48:05	1:51:21	1:54:37	1:57:54	2:01:10	2:04:27	2:07:43	2:11:00
	15	2:00:00	2:03:45	2:07:30	2:11:15	2:15:00	2:18:45	2:22:30	2:26:15	2:30:00
	18	2:24:00	2:28:30	2:33:00	2:37:30	2:42:00	2:46:30	2:51:00	2:55:30	3:00:00
	21	2:48:00	2:53:15	2:58:30	3:03:45	3:09:00	3:14:15	3:19:30	3:24:45	3:30:00
	24	3:12:00	3:18:00	3:24:00	3:30:00	3:36:00	3:42:00	3:48:00	3:54:00	4:00:00
	26.2	3:29:36	3:36:09	3:42:42	3:49:15	3:55:48	4:02:21	4:08:54	4:15:27	4:22:00

Pace (hour:min:sec per mile)									
		10:15	10:30	10:45	11:00	11:15	11:30	11:45	12:00	12:15
Distance (miles)	3	0:30:45	0:31:30	0:32:15	0:33:00	0:33:45	0:34:30	0:35:15	0:36:00	0:36:45
	6	1:01:30	1:03:00	1:04:30	1:06:00	1:07:30	1:09:00	1:10:30	1:12:00	1:13:30
	9	1:32:15	1:34:30	1:36:45	1:39:00	1:41:15	1:43:30	1:45:45	1:48:00	1:50:15
	12	2:03:00	2:06:00	2:09:00	2:12:00	2:15:00	2:18:00	2:21:00	2:24:00	2:27:00
	13.1	2:14:16	2:17:33	2:20:49	2:24:06	2:27:22	2:30:39	2:33:55	2:37:12	2:40:28
	15	2:33:45	2:37:30	2:41:15	2:45:00	2:48:45	2:52:30	2:56:15	3:00:00	3:03:45
	18	3:04:30	3:09:00	3:13:30	3:18:00	3:22:30	3:27:00	3:31:30	3:36:00	3:40:30
	21	3:35:15	3:40:30	3:45:45	3:51:00	3:56:15	4:01:30	4:06:45	4:12:00	4:17:15
	24	4:06:00	4:12:00	4:18:00	4:24:00	4:30:00	4:36:00	4:42:00	4:48:00	4:54:00
	26.2	4:28:33	4:35:06	4:41:39	4:48:12	4:54:45	5:01:18	5:07:51	5:14:24	5:20:57

Pace (hour:min:sec per mile)									
		12:30	12:45	13:00	13:15	13:30	13:45	14:00	14:30	15:00
Distance (miles)	3	0:37:30	0:38:15	0:39:00	0:39:45	0:40:30	0:41:15	0:42:00	0:43:30	0:45:00
	6	1:15:00	1:16:30	1:18:00	1:19:30	1:21:00	1:22:30	1:24:00	1:27:00	1:30:00
	9	1:52:30	1:54:45	1:57:00	1:59:15	2:01:30	2:03:45	2:06:00	2:10:30	2:15:00
	12	2:30:00	2:33:00	2:36:00	2:39:00	2:42:00	2:45:00	2:48:00	2:54:00	3:00:00
	13.1	2:43:45	2:47:01	2:50:18	2:53:34	2:56:51	3:00:08	3:03:24	3:09:57	3:16:30
	15	3:07:30	3:11:15	3:15:00	3:18:45	3:22:30	3:26:15	3:30:00	3:37:30	3:45:00
	18	3:45:00	3:49:30	3:54:00	3:58:30	4:03:00	4:07:30	4:12:00	4:21:00	4:30:00
	21	4:22:30	4:27:45	4:33:00	4:38:15	4:43:30	4:48:45	4:54:00	5:04:30	5:15:00
	24	5:00:00	5:06:00	5:12:00	5:18:00	5:24:00	5:30:00	5:36:00	5:48:00	6:00:00
	26.2	5:27:30	5:34:03	5:40:36	5:47:09	5:53:42	6:00:15	6:06:48	6:19:54	6:33:00

Acknowledgements

I want to thank my family: my husband Hugo and my children: my daughter Carolina and my sons Julian and Martin.

I would also like to thank the women who responded to my survey questions and those who shared their pictures and "how I started running" stories: Alicia Ayvas, Jenny Bohrman, Jody Bohrman, Maureen Cullen, Laura Dougherty, Laura Napolitano, Maureen McCutcheon, Anna Rowe, Stephanie Rowe and Silvia Safar. Your stories are an inspiration to all of us!

A big thank you to Jenny Bohrman, my editor. With out her, my message might have gotten lost in translation!

Thanks to Dr. Linda Stone for appearing in the picture of Strength Training Chapter page. Dr. Stone, you are also an inspiration. Also thanks to Rich Earl for taking such nice photos for the Getting Started and Injuries Chapter pages; the model (my daughter, Carolina) also helped.

Lastly, I would like to thank Ellen Seuffert, R.N., F.N.P, from Westfield Family Practice in NJ, for her time and professional advice, Jessie and David from The Westfield Running Company also for their time and expert advice, and Flavio Pardo for his advice in the Gadget section.

References

1 Byrne, A., & Byrne, D.G. (1993). The effect of exercise on depression, anxiety and other mood states: A review. *Journal of Psychosomatic Research, 37*(6), 565-574.

2 Jankauskiene, R., Kardelis, K., & Pajaujiene, S. (2005). Body weight satisfaction and weight loss attempts in fitness activity involved women. *Journal of Sports Medicine and Physical Fitness, 45*(4), 537-546.

3 Wilson, P.M., & Rodgers, W.M. (2004). The relationship between perceived autonomy support, exercise regulations and behavioral intentions in women. *Psychology of Sport and Exercise,* 5, 229-242.

4 Segar, M.L., Eccles, J.S., & Richardson, C.R. (2008). Type of physical activity goal influences participation in healthy midlife women. *Women's Health Issues,* 18, 281-291.

5 Emaus, A., Veierød, M. B., Furberg, A., Espetvedt, S., Friedenreich, C., Ellison, P.T., et al. (2008). Physical activity, heart rate, metabolic profile, and estradiol in premenopausal women. *Medicine & Science in Sports & Exercise, 40*(6), 1022-1030.

6 Chakravarthy M.V., Joyner M.J., & Booth F.W. (2002). An obligation for primary care physicians to prescribe physical activity to sedentary patients to reduce the risk of chronic health conditions. *Mayo Clinic Proceedings,* 7, 7165-73.

7 American College of Sports Medicine (2006). ACSM's Guidelines for exercise testing and prescription (7th ed.). Philadelphia, PA: Lippincott Williams & Wilkins.

8. DeLeo, A. T., Dierks, T. A., Ferber R., & Davis, I.S. (2004). Lower extremity joint coupling during running: a current update. *Clinical Biomechanics,* 19, 983–991

9 Liang, J., & Chiu, H. (2010, July). *Cushioning of the running shoes after long-term use.* Paper presented at the XXVIIIth National Society of Biomechanics in Sports Conference, Marquette, Michigan.

10 Verdejo, R. & Mills, N.J. (2004). Heel–shoe interactions and the durability of EVA foam running-shoe midsoles. *Journal of Biomechanics,* 37, 1379–1386.

11 Lieberman, D.E., Venkadesan, M., Werbel, W.A., Daoud, A.I., D'Andrea,

S., Davis, I.S., Mang'Eni, R.O., & Pitsiladis, Y. (2010). Foot strike patterns and collision forces in habitually barefoot versus shod runners. *Nature*, 463, 531-5.

12 White, J., Scurr, J., & Hedger, W. (2011). A comparison of three-dimensional breast displacement and breast comfort during overground and treadmill running. *Journal of Applied Biomechanics*, 27, 47-53.

13 McGhee, D.E., & Steele, J.R. (2006). How do respiratory state and measurement method affect bra size calculations? *British Journal of Sports Medicine*, 40, 970–974.

14 Knapik J.J., Reynolds K.L., Duplantis K.L., & Jones B.H. (1995). Friction blisters. Pathophysiology, prevention and treatment. *Sports Medicine*, 20(3), 136-47.

15 Baussan, E., Bueno, M.-A., Rossi, R.M., & Derler, S. (2010). Experiments and modeling of skin-knitted fabric friction. *Wear*, 268 1103–1110.

16 Brazaitis, M., Kamandulis, S., Skurvydas, A., & Daniuseviciute, L. (2010). The effect of two kinds of T-shirts on physiological and psychological thermal responses during exercise and recovery. *Applied Ergonomics*, 42, 46e51.

17 Storen, O., Helgerud, J., & Hoff, J. (2011). Running Stride Peak Forces Inversely Determine Running Economy in Elite Runners. *Journal of Strength and Conditioning Research*, 25(1), 117-123.

18 Keller, T. S., Weisberger, A. M., Ray, J. L., Hasan, S. S., Shiavi, R. G., & Spengler, D. M. (1996). Relationship between vertical ground reaction force and speed during walking, slow jogging, and running. *Clinical Biomechanics*, 11(5), 253-259.

19 "Dietary Guidelines for Americans," 2010. Retrieved December 2011 from http://health.gov/dietaryguidelines/dga2010/DietaryGuidelines2010.pdf

20 Brown-Kramer C. R., Kiviniemi M. T., & Winseman J. A., (2010). Food exemplar salience: What foods do people think of when you tell them to change their diet? *Appetite*, 52(3), 753–756.

21 Büchner, F. L. Bueno-de-Mesquita, H. B., Linseisen, J., Boshuizen, H. C., Kiemeney,L. A. L. M., Ros, M. M., … Riboli, E. (2010). Fruits and vegetables consumption and the risk of histological subtypes of lung cancer in the European Prospective Investigation into Cancer and Nutrition (EPIC). *Cancer Causes Control*, 2(13) 357–371.

22 "Beans and other legumes: Types and cooking tips," Retrieved December 2011 from http://www.mayoclinic.com/health/legumes/NU00260

23 "Food exchange list," 2012. Retrieved January 2012 from http://www.nhlbi.nih.gov/health/public/heart/obesity/lose_wt/fd_exch.htm#5

24 Sizer, F., & Whitney E. (2000). Nutrition: concepts and controversies. 8th ed. Wadsworth/Thompson Learning, CA.

25 "If olive oil is high in fat, why is it considered healthy?," 2011. Retrieved December 2011 from http://www.mayoclinic.com/health/food-and-nutrition/AN01037

26 "A Key to Choosing Healthful Foods: Using the Nutrition Facts on the Food Label," 2011. Retrieved December 2011 from http://www.fda.gov/Food/ResourcesForYou/Consumers/ucm079449.htm

27 Gao, X., Wilde, P.E., Lichtenstein, A.H., Bermudez, O. I., & Tucker, K. L. (2002). The maximal amount of dietary alpha-tocopherol intake in US adults. *Journal of Nutrition, 136*(4), 1021-1026.

28 Lonn E, Bosch J, Yusuf S, Sheridan P, Pogue J, Arnold J.M, … Dagenais G.R. (2005). Effects of long-term vitamin E supplementation on cardiovascular events and cancer: a randomized controlled trial. *The Journal of the American Medical Association, 293* 1338–47.

29 Miller, 3rd ER, Pastor-Barriuso R, Dalal D, Riemersma RA, Appel LJ, & Guallar E. (2005). Meta-analysis: high-dosage vitamin E supplementation may increase all-cause mortality. *Annuals of Internal Medicine, 142*(1), 37-46.

30 Barreiro-Hurlé, J., Gracia, A., & de-Magistris, T. (2010). Does nutrition information on food products lead to healthier food choices? *Food Policy, 35*(3), 221-229.

31 Colby, S. E., Johnson, LA., Scheett, A., & Hoverson, B. (2010). Nutrition Marketing on Food Labels. *Journal of Nutrition Education and Behavior, 42*(2), 92-98, ISSN 1499-4046, 10.1016/j.jneb.2008.11.002.

32 Bowman, S. A. (2005). Food shoppers' nutrition attitudes and relationship to dietary and lifestyle practices. *Nutrition Research*, 25 281–293.

33 "Overnight Oatmeal," Retrieved January 2010 from http://www.foodnetwork.com/recipes/alton-brown/overnight-oatmeal-recipe/index.html

34 Kubukeli, Z. N., Noakes T. D., & Dennis S. C. (2002). Training techniques to improve endurance exercise performances. *Sports Medicine, 32*(8), 489-509.

35 "More/Fitness Half-Marathon- Race Statistics," 2011. Retrieved February 2010 from http://web2.nyrrc.org/cgi-bin/htmlos.cgi/4358.1.449499096312857545

36 "Nike 26.2 = Nike Women's Marathon - Race Results," 2011. Retrieved February 2010 from http://www.marathonguide.com/results/browse.cfm?MIDD=2224121014

37 Jeukendrup A. E., Jentjens R. L., & Moseley L. (2005). Nutritional considerations in triathlon. *Sports Medicine, 35*(2), 163-181.

38 Ganio, M. S., Casa, D. J., Armstrong, L. E., & Maresh, C. M. (2007). Evidence-based approach to lingering hydration questions. *Clinics in Sport Medicine, 26*, 1-16.

39 Ali, A., Duizer, L., Foster, K., Grigor, J., & Wei, W. (2011). Changes in sensory perception of sports drinks when consumed pre, during and post exercise. *Physiology & Behavior,* 102, 437–443.

40 Goodsell T. L., & Harris, B. D. (2011). Family Life and Marathon Running: Constraint, Cooperation, and Gender in a Leisure Activity. *Journal of Leisure Research, 43* (1), 80-109.

41 Korpela, K. & Kinnunen U. (2010): How Is Leisure Time Iteracting with Nature Related to the Need for Recovery from Work Demands? Testing Multiple Mediators, *Leisure Sciences, 33*(1), 1-14.

42 American College of Sports Medicine Position Stand (2011). Quantity and Quality of Exercise for Developing and Maintaining Cardiorespiratory, Musculoskeletal, and Neuromotor Fitness in Apparently Healthy Adults: Guidance for Prescribing Exercise. *Medicine & Science in Sports & Exercise*, 0195-9131/11/4307-1334/0.

43 Maschi, R., Williams, H. (2009). *A Runner's Guide to Plyometrics and Core Strength Training.* NY, NY, Print.

44 Snyder, K. R., Earl, J. E., O'Connor, K. M., & Ebersole, K. T. (2009). Resistance training is accompanied by increases in hip strength and changes in lower extremity biomechanics during running. *Clinical Biomechanics, 24*(1), 26-34.

45 Grivas G., Soulas D., Manou V., Voutselas V., & Papanikolaou Z. (2009). Strength training in middle and long distance running. *Inquiries in Sport & Physical Education 7*(2), 244 - 253.

46 National Strength and Conditioning Association (2008). *Essentials of strength training and conditioning (3ʳᵈ ed.).* Champaign, IL: Human Kinetics.

47 Burnett, D., & Smith, K., Smeltzer C., Young K., Burns, S. (2010). Perceived muscle soreness in recreational female runners. *International Journal of Exercise Science,. 3*(3), 108-116.

48 Gilchrist J., Jones B. H., Sleet D. A., & Kimsey C. D. (2000). Exercise-related injuries among women: strategies for prevention from civilian and military studies. *Recommendations and reports: Morbidity and mortality weekly report. Recommendations and reports / Centers for Disease Control, 49* (2) 15-33.

49 Bischof, J. E., Abbey, A. N., Chuckpaiwong, B., Nunley, J. A., & Queen, R. M. (2010). Three-dimensional ankle kinematics and kinetics during running in women. *Gait & Posture,* 31 502–505.

50 Blackman, P. (2010). Shin pain in athletes: Assessment and management. *Australian Family Physician, 39,* 1/2, 24-29.

51 Fields, K.B., Sykes, J.C., Walker, K.M., & Jackson J.C. (2010). Prevention of running injuries. *Current Sports Medicine Report, 9*(3),176-182.

52 Owens, S. C., & Humphries, W. T. (2011). Femoral shaft stress fracture in a female recreational runner. *International Journal Of Athletic Therapy & Training, 16*(1), 21-23.

53 Tonoti, C., Cumps, E. Aert, I., Verhagen, E., Meeusen, R. (2010). Incidence, risk factors and prevention of running related injuries in long-distance running: a systematic review Injury, location and type. *Sport & Medicine, 5,* 12-18.

54 Strakowski, J. A. & Jamil, T. (2006). Management of common running injuries. *Physical Medicine and Rehabilitation Clinics of North America, 17*(3), 537-552.

55 Wilder, R. P., & Sethi, S. (2004). Overuse injuries: Tendinopathies, stress fractures, compartment syndrome, and shin splints. *Clinics in Sports Medicine, 23*(1), 55-81.

56 Paluska S. A. (2005). An overview of hip injuries in running. *Sports Medicine, 35*(11) , 991-1014.

57 Peake, S., Manderson, L., & Potts, H. (1999). "Part and parcel of being a woman": Female urinary incontinence and constructions of control. *Medical Anthropology Quarterly, New Series, 13* (3), 267-285.

58 Danforth, K. N., Townsend, M. K., Lifford, K., Curhan, G. C., Resnick, N. M., & Grodstein, F. (2006). Risk factors for urinary incontinence among middle-aged women. *American Journal of Obstetrics and Gynecology,* 194, 339–45.

59 Townsend, M. K., Danforth, K. N., Lifford, K. L., Rosner, B., Curhan, G. C., Resnick, N. M., et al. (2007). Incidence and remission of urinary incontinence in middleaged women. *American Journal of Obstetric and Gynecology,* 197, 167.e1-167.e5.

60 Nygaard, I. E., Kreder, K. J., Lepic, M. M., Fountain, K. A., & Rhomberg, A. T. (1995). Efficacy of pelvic floor muscle exercises in urge, and mixed urinary incontinence women. *American Journal of Obstetric and Gynecology, 174* (1), 121-125.

61 Peeker, I. & Peeker, R. (2003). Early diagnosis and treatment of genuine stress urinary incontinence in women after pregnancy: Midwives as detectives. *American College of Nurse-Midwives, 48* (1), 60-66.

62 Pfeiffer, B., Cotterill, A., Grathwohl, D., Steliingwerff, T., & Jeukendrup, A. E. (2009). The Effect of Carbohydrate Gels on Gastrointestinal Tolerance During a 16-km Run. *International Journal of Sport Nutrition and Exercise Metabolism,* 19, 485-503.

63 Strid, H., & Simrén, M. (2005). The effects of physical activity on the gastrointestinal tract. *International Sports Medicine Journal, 6* (3), 151-161.

64 Shi, X., Horn, M. K., Osterberg, K. L., Stofan, J. R., Zachwieja, J. J.,

Horswill, C. A., Passe, D. H. & Murray, R. (2004). Gastrointestinal discomfort during intermittent high-intensity exercise: Effect of carbohydrate–electrolyte beverage. *International Journal of Sport Nutrition and Exercise Metabolism,* 14, 673-683.

65 Latzka, W. A., & Montain, S. J. (1999). Water and electrolyte requirements for exercise. *Clinics in Sports Medicine, 18*(3), 513-524.

66 Noakes, T.D. (1993). Fluid replacement during exercise. Holloszy J (ed): *Exercise and Sport Sciences Reviews,* 21, 297-330.

67 Seto, C. K., Way, D., & O'Connor, N. (2005). Environmental illness in athletes. *Clinics in Sports Medicine*, 24, 695-718.

68 Mailler-Savage, E. A. & Adams, B. B. (2006). Skin manifestations of running. *Journal of the American Academy of Dermatology,* 55, 290-301.

69 Knapik J. J, Reynolds K. L, Duplantis K. L, & Jones B.H. (1995). Friction blisters. Pathophysiology, prevention and treatment. *Journal of Sports Medicine, 20* (3)136–147.

70 Knapik, J.J., Reynolds, K.L., Duplantis, K.L., & Jones, B.H. (1995). Friction blisters. Pathophysiology, prevention and treatment. *Journal of Sports Medicine, 20*(3), 136-47.

71 Pharis D. B, Teller, C, & Wolf, J. E. (1997). Cutaneous manifestations of sports participation. *Journal of the American Academy of Dermatology,* 36, 448-59.

72 Armstrong, B. & Kricker, A. (1993). How much melanoma is caused by sun exposure? *Melanoma Research*, 3(6), 395–401.

73 Moehrle, M. (2008). Outdoor sports and skin cancer. *Clinics in Dermatology, 26*(1), 12-15.

74 Douglas Stern, personal communication, Deep water running results, Dec. 2004.

75 Kilding, A. E., Scott, M. A., & Mullineaux, D. R. (2007). A kinematic comparison of deep water running and overground running in endurance runners. *Journal of Strength And Conditioning Research, 21*(2), 476-480.

76 Joubert, D. P., Oden, G. L., & Estes, B. C. (2011). The Effects of Elliptical Cross Training on VO_2 max in Recently Trained Runners. *International Journal of Exercise Science 4*(1) 243-251.

77 Leyk D., Rüther T., Wunderlich M., Sievert, A., Eßfeld, D., Witzki, A., … Löllgen, H. (2010). Physical performance in middle age and Old age: good news for our sedentary and aging society. *Deutsches Ärzteblatt International, 107*(46) 809–16. DOI:10.3238/ arztebl.2010.0809.

78 Celie, F., Faes, M., Hopman, M., Stalenhoef, A. F. H., & Olde Rikkert, M. G. M. (2010). Running on age in a 15-km road run: minor influence of age on performance. *European Review of Aging and Physical Activity,* 7, 43–47.

79 Brooks, G. A., Fahey, T. D., & Baldwin, K. M. (2005). *Exercise physiology: Human biogenetics and its applications* (4th ed.). New York, NY: McGraw-Hill.

80 Froese, G., and A. C. Burton (1957). Heat losses from the human head. *Journal of Applied. Physiology,* 10, 235-241.